100
SIMPLE SECRETS
OF
HAPPY
PEOPLE

Also in this series

100
SIMPLE SECRETS
OF
HAPPY
PEOPLE

WHAT SCIENTISTS HAVE LEARNED
AND HOW YOU CAN USE IT

DAVID NIVEN, Ph.D.

HarperOne
An Imprint of HarperCollinsPublishers

HarperCollins books may be purchased for educational, business, or sales promotional use. For information please write: Special Markets Department, HarperCollins Publishers, 10 East 53rd Street, New York, NY 10022.

HarperCollins Web site: http://www.harpercollins.com

HarperCollins®, ✦®, and HarperOne™
are trademarks of HarperCollins Publishers.

Library of Congress Cataloging-in-Publication Data
Niven, David, Ph.D.
100 simple secrets of happy people: what scientists have
learned and how you can use it / David Niven. — 1st ed.
p. cm.
Includes bibliographical references.
ISBN: 978-0-06-115791-2
1. Happiness. 2. Conduct of life. I. Title: One hundred simple secrets
of happy people. II. Title.
BJ1481.N58   2000
158—dc21   99-087647

08 09 10 11 CW 10 9

TO

T.O.

Contents

A Note to Readers

Each of the 100 entries presented here is based on the research conclusions of scientists studying happiness and life satisfaction. Each entry contains a key research finding, complemented by advice and an example that follow from the finding. The research conclusions presented in each entry are based on a meta-analysis of research on happiness, which means that each conclusion is derived from the work of multiple researchers studying the same topic. To enable the reader to find further information on each topic, a reference to a supporting study is included in each entry, and a bibliography of recent work on happiness has also been provided.

Introduction

Harry Gilman has spent his career studying people, and he knows that often what many people want and need is right in front of their faces, if only they could see it.

"No one can snap their fingers and make someone happy. What you can do is help people to see what is useful for them to see. What you can do is point and hope they look."

Harry Gilman is a psychology professor. He could have carved a fine existence out of publishing academic research and lecturing on that research to his colleagues. But unlike many professors, Harry didn't see his job as publishing scientific papers for scientific readers. He said in a seminar one time, "What would be the point of finding out something and then never telling anyone who could really use the information? Why play 'I've got a secret' your entire life? Psychology professors who figure out a better way to think about life spend their careers sharing it with other professors."

One of the many things that made Harry an extraordinary teacher was that he cared. In his psychology seminars, he required every student to submit a notebook—a bound, marbleized notebook, to be exact—every week. In it we were told to write something, anything. What did we think about? What were our concerns? What were our hopes, fears? These were the questions the students returned to week after week.

We were so taken with the process that many of us shared our notebooks with one another. Max Leer, one of my classmates, almost always wrote about his relationship with his father, a man who never seemed satisfied with his life or with Max.

Harry would read our entries closely and comment on them. To Max, Harry wrote, "Max, for some people there are no victories, just alternate forms of losing."

That phrase never left me. It was a powerful way of sending home the point that Harry had been making in class: much in life is simply a matter of perspective. It's not inherently good or bad, a success or failure; it's how we choose to look at things that makes the difference.

"What do you make of life? That's the question," Harry said to the class. "Sugar, flour, and eggs—are they good or bad? You could make of them a cake, or you could just make a mess. But then that cake, or that mess—is it good or bad? Can you make it good? Of course. Can you make it bad? Certainly."

Another day, Harry impressed upon me and my classmates what he called the nearly boundless capacity of humans to ignore the long-term implications of their decisions while they focus on short-term effects. He spoke of the difference between an impartial, logical observer, who would always make long-term decisions, and the person who can't see beyond their immediate gratification. "A child will always reach for the lollipop; only the adult watching thinks tooth decay and lack of nutrition," Harry said. "We have to strive to be the adult watching above, not just living the moment, but seeing from outside ourselves what is happening, what should be happening, what things we are doing that will ultimately hurt us."

Harry's classes interested us, and Harry inspired us. With graduation fast approaching, our conversation often drifted to the subject of our futures and career choices. "What can you do with psychology?" Harry asked us rhetorically. "All we can do is give out the best answers we have. Then people have a chance to use them."

On graduation day, I went up to Harry to shake his hand. "I don't know how to thank you, Harry. You made me a better person."

"Thank you, David," Harry responded, "but I didn't make you a better person. All I can do is point and hope you look."

I offer you *100 Simple Secrets of Happy People* in that spirit—pointing to findings of psychological research on happy people, and hoping you will look.

What do happy people do differently than unhappy people? Psychology's best observations appear in academic journals like the *Journal of Personality and Social Psychology* and the *Journal of Applied Behavioral Science.* But you may not have access to these journals, and even if you did, you would find them written in scientific gobbledygook, not understandable English.

That's where *100 Simple Secrets of Happy People* comes in. After reviewing over a thousand studies written during the last decade exploring the characteristics and beliefs of happy people, I have taken the best, most practical advice from that body of research. Instead of using academic jargon, *100 Simple Secrets of Happy People* translates the conclusions of this research into simple, useful advice.

Each study on happiness has been boiled down to its core and then expressed in a way everyone will understand. With the scientific results of research as its foundation, *100 Simple Secrets of Happy People* offers 100 simple pieces of advice and examples of how people find happiness and stay happy.

The *100 Simple Secrets of Happy People* is not just one person's intuition. Rather, it reflects the research conclusions of noted scientists studying the lives of regular people. My interpretation and translation of this research will help those who want to know more about the differences between happy and unhappy people. It will also help those who want to know what they can do to enjoy life more. I'm pointing now, and I hope you will look.

Your Life Has Purpose and Meaning

You are not here just to fill space or to be a background character in someone else's movie.

Consider this: nothing would be the same if you did not exist. Every place you have ever been and everyone you have ever spoken to would be different without you.

We are all connected, and we are all affected by the decisions and even the existence of those around us.

TAKE THE EXAMPLE of Peter, an attorney in Philadelphia, and his dog, Tucket. Tucket was very sick. Gradually he was becoming paralyzed by a tumor on his spinal cord.

Peter could not find a veterinary doctor who could save his dog. Desperate to find someone who could help, he turned to a pediatric neurosurgeon. The doctor agreed to try to help Tucket, and in return he asked Peter for a donation to the children's hospital he worked in.

Jerry has never met Peter or Tucket. Jerry is a blue-eyed, blond-haired, five-year-old boy who loves to eat mashed potatoes. Jerry also has tumors on his spine and in his brain.

With help from the donation Peter made to the hospital, Jerry underwent successful surgery performed by the doctor to remove the tumors.

Tucket's surgery was also a success.

Studies of older Americans find that one of the best predictors of happiness is whether a person considers his or her life to have a purpose. Without a clearly defined purpose, seven in ten individuals feel unsettled about their lives; with a purpose, almost seven in ten feel satisfied. (Lepper 1996)

Use a Strategy for Happiness

We assume that happy and unhappy people are born that way. But both kinds of people do things that create and reinforce their moods. Happy people let themselves be happy. Unhappy people continue doing things that upset them.

WHAT IS THE first sign of a healthy business? A healthy business plan. That is the argument of the Strategic Management Center, a business consulting firm. They believe every business must define its purpose and then create a strategy to accomplish that purpose.

This same approach can be used by people. Define what you want, then use a strategy to get it.

Ironically, children are better at this than adults. Small children know when being cranky will get them an ice cream cone. And they know when being too noisy will get them a cross reaction from their parents. Children understand that there are rules and predictable patterns to life, and they use a strategy to help them get what they want.

Living a happy life as an adult is like trying to get that ice cream cone as a child. You need to know what you want and use a strategy to get it. Think about what makes you happy and what makes you sad, and use this to help you get what you want.

Happy people do not experience one success after another and unhappy people, one failure after another. Instead, surveys show that happy and unhappy people tend to have had very similar life experiences. The difference is that the average unhappy person spends more than twice as much time thinking about unpleasant events in their lives, while happy people tend to seek and rely upon information that brightens their personal outlook. (Lyubomirsky 1994)

You Don't Have to Win Every Time

Ultracompetitive people, who always need to win, end up enjoying things less. If they lose they are very disappointed, and if they win it's what they expected would happen anyway.

RICHARD NIXON WAS running for reelection as president in 1972. He directed his campaign staff to take all available measures to win as many votes as possible. Most famous, of course, were the break-ins they staged at Democratic Party headquarters in the Watergate building in order to plant bugging devices. But staff workers also engaged in an endless series of what Nixon himself labeled "dirty tricks." They would call up pizza parlors and order a hundred pizzas to be delivered to the office of an opposition candidate. They would hand out phony fliers telling people that an opponent's rally had been canceled. They would call meeting halls and cancel reservations opponents had made for events. Why did they do these things? Nixon was obsessed with winning—at all costs.

The great irony was that Nixon was winning anyway and didn't need any of these tricks. But his inability to deal with the possibility of losing caused him to pursue these extreme methods and ultimately cost him the prize that he had so desperately pursued.

Competitiveness can preclude life satisfaction because no accomplishment can prove sufficient, and failures are particularly devastating. Ultracompetitive people rate their successes with lower marks than some people rate their failures. (Thurman 1981)

Your Goals Should Be Aligned with One Another

The four tires of your car have to be properly aligned; otherwise the left tires will be pointed in a different direction from the right tires and the car won't work. Goals are just like that. They all must be pointed in the same direction. If your goals conflict with one another, your life may not work.

JORGE RAMOS WAS on the fast track in television news. He anchored a broadcast that could be seen in the United States and Latin America. He covered major political figures and jumped at the chance to cover wars—and risk his life—in the Middle East, Latin America, and Europe.

Ramos was doing exceptionally well by his own calculations, both professionally and economically. He wished to push his career even further. He wanted to "peer into the hearts of those that dominate the planet and be at the places where history changes."

But Ramos was also missing his family, all the time. When he was away from home, viewing a picture of his daughter could make him cry as he thought about the time apart, the distance, the danger that he had exposed himself to and the effect that could have on her.

Ramos eventually realized he could not keep his goal of being where the action was and being where he needed to be most—with his family.

In a long-term study of subjects over the course of more than a decade, life satisfaction was associated with the consistency of life goals. Goals regarding career, education, family, and geography were each important, and together add up to about 80 percent of satisfaction. These goals need to be consistent with one another to produce positive conclusions regarding goal achievement. (Wilson, Henry, and Peterson 1997)

Choose Your Comparisons Wisely

Many of our feelings of satisfaction or dissatisfaction have their roots in how we compare ourselves to others. When we compare ourselves to those who have more, we feel bad. When we compare ourselves to those who have less, we feel grateful. Even though the truth is we have exactly the same life either way, our feelings about our life can vary tremendously based on who we compare ourselves with. Compare yourself with those examples that are meaningful but that make you feel comfortable with who you are and what you have.

JOE IS THE OLDEST of six brothers. The brothers range in age from twenty-one to forty-two. His family never had a lot of money, and the older brothers especially grew up in modest circumstances. When they finished high school, Joe and the two older brothers went to work. When the three younger brothers finished high school, however, they went to college. The older brothers feel like they missed out. Since financial aid wasn't as plentiful, they really didn't have a chance to get more education.

If they compare themselves to their younger brothers, Joe and the older brothers may feel disappointment and jealousy. They may ask, Why did they get opportunities I did not? But if they compare themselves to many of their friends—men their age, men who had similar opportunities—the brothers see that they have more than most of their friends in terms of job satisfaction and a fulfilling family life.

Of course, Joe would gain no advantage by depriving his younger siblings of their opportunities. But he still feels bad when he compares himself to them. The answer, then, is not to make that comparison. The younger brothers grew up two decades later, in a different world and in many respects in a different family. Instead of disappointing themselves by making this comparison, Joe and the older brothers can feel good about both their younger brothers and themselves when they make a more realistic comparison to those who faced the same challenges as they did.

A large group of students was given a word puzzle to solve. Researchers compared the satisfaction of students who finished the puzzle quickly or more slowly. Students who finished the puzzle quickly and compared themselves with the very fastest students came away feeling dissatisfied with themselves. Students who finished the puzzle more slowly but compared themselves with the slowest students came away feeling quite satisfied with themselves and tended to ignore the presence of the quick-finishing students. (Lyubomirsky and Ross 1997)

Cultivate Friendships

Rekindle past relationships, and take advantage of opportunities at work or among your neighbors to expand your friendship base. People need to feel that they are a part of something bigger, that they care about others and are cared about by others in return.

ANDY DIDN'T REALLY know his neighbors. He would wave if he saw them in the yard, but mainly what he saw were tall fences and closed doors.

Andy had bought himself a computer a few years ago, intending to use it for his job. Goofing off one day, he found himself exploring the Internet. Andy visited various sites where people with common interests in books or sports or art gathered online to discuss their hobbies.

He fell into conversation with one particular person during his computer journey and soon found that they had much in common and thoroughly enjoyed conversing (albeit through a computer) with each other.

Weeks later, during a computer conversation with this new friend, Andy's house lost electrical power, shutting down his computer and cutting off his link to his friend. When the electricity came back on, Andy searched for his friend only to find that the friend, at the very same time, had also been cut off because of an electrical outage.

Suspicious about the coincidence, Andy and the friend decided to divulge their locations. Of all the places in the world the two of them could have been—with the computer capable of linking people on different continents, even on different sides of the Earth—it turned out that Andy and his friend lived on the very same street! When electricity went off on the street, it went off at both of their houses, which were just doors away from each other.

The lesson Andy learned is that there are wonderful people out there but also wonderful people right here—if you just take the opportunity to get to know them.

Close relationships, more than personal satisfaction or one's view of the world as a whole, are the most meaningful factors in happiness. If you feel close to other people, you are four times as likely to feel good about yourself than if you do not feel close to anyone. (Magen, Birenbaum, and Pery 1996)

Turn Off the TV

Television is a creamy filling that distracts us from the substance of our lives.

WHEN YOU ARE in the supermarket, do you buy something from each and every aisle? Of course not. You go to aisles that have something you want and skip the aisles that don't have anything you need. But when it comes to watching television, many of us seem to follow the buy-something-from-every-aisle plan. If it's Monday, we watch TV. If it's Tuesday, we watch TV. If it's Wednesday, we watch TV. Too often we watch TV because that's what we usually do rather than because there is something we actually want to see. Ask yourself when you are watching TV, "Is this something I want to see? Would I ask that this program be made if it didn't already exist?"

Psychologists have found some people who watch so much TV that it actually inhibits their ability to carry on a conversation. In the words of one psychologist, "TV robs our time and never gives it back."

Don't turn on the TV just because it's there and that's what you usually do. Turn it on only when there is something on that you want to watch. Your newly liberated hours can be spent doing something with your family or your friends or finding a rare quiet moment for yourself.

Without TV, you can do something actively fun instead of passively distracting.

Watching too much TV can triple our hunger for more possessions, while reducing our personal contentment by about 5 percent for every hour a day we watch. (Wu 1998)

Accept Yourself—Unconditionally

Y ou are not just the size of your bank account, the neighborhood you live in, or the type of work you do. You are, just like everyone else, an almost inconceivably complicated mix of abilities and limitations.

A NEW KIND of New Year's resolution is becoming increasingly popular. Instead of dwelling on something they think is wrong with them and resolving to improve, a lot of people are taking a different approach. They are resolving to accept themselves. To acknowledge that, faults and all, they are complete people, good people.

Kathleen, a member of a group that spreads the acceptance philosophy, explains that she used to feel like she was in a trap she could not get out of. She would try to correct herself and change herself, and the failure to change was actually worse than the original problem itself. She felt like a "maniac" because of the pressures to change and the weight of failure.

Now Kathleen counsels accepting yourself, which does not mean ignoring your faults or never trying to improve. What it does mean is "believing in your own value first, last, and always."

In a study of adult self-esteem, researchers found that people who are happy with themselves take defeat and explain it away, treating it as an isolated incident that indicates nothing about their ability. People who are unhappy take defeat and enlarge it, making it stand for who they are and using it to predict the outcome of future life events. (Brown and Dutton 1995)

Remember Where You Came From

Think about and celebrate your ethnicity. Often we feel lost in a vast and complex world. There is tremendous comfort in knowing your ethnic heritage. It gives you a history, a sense of place, a uniqueness that remains no matter what else is going on around you.

OUR HOMES LOOK the same, our towns look the same, we watch the same movies, we dress the same, we often seem indistinguishable from everyone else. We live in a time of massproduced everything, and we often feel lost in all the sameness. We long to know how we fit into the world. Where did I come from, and how did I get to this place? Knowing our family history and our ethnic heritage can offer comfort because it helps tell us who we are, where we're from, and how we fit.

The Foundation for Empowerment is one good example. The group teaches African American children about their heritage with history lessons, art lessons, and celebrations of food and music.

What do the students get out of these lessons? Pride. A sense of accomplishment. A sense of place. The effects are impressive. Students who participate tend to improve both their attendance and grades in school. As one eighth-grader explained, the program has made her work harder, be more committed to a professional career goal, and "feel better about myself because I know more about my heritage."

In studies of students, greater ethnic identity is associated with 10 percent greater life satisfaction. (Neto 1995)

Limit Yourself to Thinking About One Subject as You Lie Down to Sleep

Those who have a lot of anxiety let their thoughts shoot around from one subject to another as they try to go to sleep until, in a matter of minutes, they have created a virtual catalogue of problems. With all these problems, you'll ask yourself, how can I possibly sleep?

Tonight as you are brushing your teeth, come up with something you'd like to think about when you slip under the covers. If other thoughts start to intrude, guide yourself back to that one subject.

MEGAN HATES JUNK mail. Not only does it waste her time, it also creates garbage. There's so much garbage! Megan doesn't know how people can throw out so much stuff. They say the landfills are nearly full.

Where will the garbage go then? It's not just garbage. There's all the waste from nuclear plants and toxic chemicals. What will the environment be like for the next generation? In two generation? Will the Earth survive? Can it possibly?

Too many of us allow our presleep thoughts to drift like this. Here Megan's minor annoyance leads to concerns about the future of the planet. And those concerns race around, causing stress instead of relaxation and sending people like Megan in search of sleep aids.

Too many thoughts, we now know, even if they don't lead to such a drastic topic as the fate of the Earth, are unsettling and make it much harder to sleep. When our thoughts bounce in and out, each idea backed by another, the stream of ideas makes us more on edge and less ready to close our eyes, shut off our brain for the day, and fall blissfully into sleep.

In studies of college students, shifting between pre-sleep thoughts was found to be related to difficulty in sleeping and lower sleep quality, which, in turn, were related to unhappiness. Better sleepers are 6 percent more satisfied with their lives than average sleepers, and 25 percent more satisfied than poor sleepers. (Abdel Khalek, Al-Meshaan, and Al-Shatti 1995)

Friendship Beats Money

If you want to know if people are happy, don't ask them how much money they have in the bank. Don't ask how large their take-home salary is. Ask them about their friends.

TWO FINANCIAL ADVISERS were in business together for over a decade, and then the market turned sour. They put everything they had into the business, but it wasn't enough, and soon they lost their business and all their money. When it was time to pick up the pieces, they both dwelled on the lost money and, in the process, lost their friendship.

Each blamed the other for the financial disaster. After not speaking to each other for over a year, though, they met each other for lunch. They both admitted to the other that they had experienced a major loss. And it wasn't the money, it was their friendship. One of them said, "Money is like a glove. Friendship is like your hand. One is useful, the other essential."

Contrary to the belief that happiness is hard to explain, or that it depends on having great wealth, researchers have identified the core factors in a happy life. The primary components are number of friends, closeness of friends, closeness of family, and relationships with co-workers and neighbors. Together these features explain about 70 percent of personal happiness. (Murray and Peacock 1996)

Have Realistic Expectations

People who are happy don't get everything they want, but they want most of what they get. In other words, they rig the game in their favor by choosing to value things that are within their grasp.

People who find themselves dissatisfied in life often set unreachable goals for themselves, setting themselves up to fail. Yet people who set high goals for themselves and reach them are no happier than people who set and reach more modest goals.

Whether you are assessing your position at work or your relationship with your family, don't begin with fantasy pictures of the world's richest person or the world's ideal family. Stay with reality and strive to make things better, not perfect.

THERE WAS A BIG retirement party for a high school principal, celebrating his thirty years of service to the Altoona, Pennsylvania, schools. People spoke eloquently of his wonderful contribution to thousands of children's education. At the end of the night of testimonials, he said to his friend, "When I was twenty three, I thought I was eventually going to be president of the United States."

Here was a man who was universally respected, who had given himself to the vital calling of education, and who had risen through the ranks to lead a high school. And instead of reveling in his accomplishments, he was resigned to his defeats. He was by no means a failure—he was the opposite of failure—but in comparison with his immense and unreachable goals, he could not enjoy his success.

The congruence of people's goals with their resources strongly correlates with happiness. In other words, the more realistic and attainable people's goals are, the more likely they are to feel good about themselves. People who conclude their goals are out of reach are less than one-tenth as likely to consider themselves satisfied with life. (Diener and Fujita 1995)

13

Be Open to New Ideas

Never stop learning and adapting. The world will always be changing. If you limit yourself to what you knew and what you were comfortable with earlier in your life, you will grow increasingly frustrated with your surroundings as you age.

YOU WOULD SEE him around town from time to time. People knew him only as Herb. He was always walking by the side of the road. People asked him why he was always walking, and Herb told them he didn't believe in moving machines. Didn't own a car, wouldn't own a car, wouldn't take a cab or a bus.

Why? He said he got along just fine without them when he was younger, so why should he bother with them now? This belief provided him momentary comfort. He did not have to adapt, to face a change that he feared. However, he also shut himself off from everything that was not within a few miles of his house.

The world might as well not have existed for him, as he could not directly experience anything outside of his hometown. Principles are valuable and should be cherished, but there is a difference between principle and stubborn practice. As time went on and the lives of his children led them to scatter across the country, Herb consigned himself to never being able to visit them because he refused to adapt to the world as it exists.

In research on older Americans, what predicted satisfaction more than finances or the state of their current relationships was their willingness to adapt. If they were willing to change some of their habits and expectations, their happiness was maintained even when their circumstances changed. Those who were resistant to change, on the other hand, were less than one-third as likely to feel happy. (Clark, Carlson, Zemke, Gelya, Patterson, and Ennevor 1996)

14

Share with Others How Important They Are to You

Relationships are built on mutual appreciation, and there is no better way to show that appreciation than to tell someone how much you care.

RESEARCHERS AT THE University of Houston have studied the question of why we don't tell people how important they are to us. One area they studied was reaction to sad events like funerals.

One subject, Bill, lost a close family member recently. Some of Bill's friends sent sympathy cards, some sent flowers, some sent notes, some told him they were there for him. And some did nothing.

Why did some of his friends not say anything?

Perhaps they thought that telling others we care means being vulnerable. For these people, relationships may be more of a competition than a celebration, and competitions are premised on strength, power, and position.

Researchers caution that we don't win at relationships, we win by having relationships.

Research on unemployed adults has found that the length of unemployment was less important to a person's self-esteem than the amount of social support received from parents, family members, and friends. (Lackovic-Grgin and Dekovic 1996)

15

If You're Not Sure, Guess Positively

Unhappy people take a situation in which they are not sure and come to a negative conclusion. For example, if they aren't certain why another person is being nice, they assume that the person must have a hidden selfish agenda. Happy people take that same situation and guess the positive possibility, that is, that the person really is nice.

HENRY IS A seventy-year-old man who always had a good word for his neighbors. He lived modestly in Arkansas in a small home with only a wood stove for heat. Over the years, Henry watched his home deteriorate steadily. But he was too old and had too little money to fix it up. One of his neighbors organized a group to virtually rebuild Henry's house, giving it modern heat and plumbing. Henry was stunned by this. Why were all these people taking such an interest in him, in his house? He initially wondered, What did they stand to gain? Were they trying to change his house so that it would make their houses worth more?

Any situation can be viewed as an act of selfishness, if that's how you want to view it. Taking this perspective makes us cold, critical, and cynical. And there's no way out of it, because a person we view negatively cannot do anything to improve our impression of them. We need to consider that our perspective on what motivates people can either be a source of comfort to us or a source of alarm.

Henry's ultimate conclusion: "These were just good people doing a good thing, and I thank them for it."

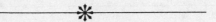

Happy people and unhappy people explain the world differently. When an unhappy person must interpret the world, eight in ten times he or she will see the negative in an event. When a happy person must interpret the world, eight in ten times he or she will see the positive. (Brebner 1995)

Believe in Yourself

Don't write yourself off. If you don't believe in yourself, you won't be able to function.

STEVE BLASS WAS a great major league pitcher in 1972. In fact, he was one of the very best. One year later, he was on his way out of baseball. Did he get hurt? No. Did anything change?

One thing changed: Steve Blass lost his confidence. As Blass said, "When it was gone, it was gone for good." He started thinking about all the things that could go wrong, and suddenly they did. Steve Blass no longer believed he could be a major league pitcher, and before he knew it, he no longer was a major league pitcher.

The ability to do anything must be accompanied by the belief that we *can* do it. As important as learning how is learning that you know how. There is an old saying, "Whether you believe you can or you believe you can't, either way you're right."

Across all ages and all groups, a solid belief in one's own abilities increases life satisfaction by about 30 percent, and makes us happier both in our home lives and in our work lives. (Myers and Diener 1995)

Don't Believe in Yourself Too Much

Believing in yourself means thinking you are a capable person, not that you will never make a mistake. Don't think that because you are a talented person you cannot learn from others or you should never be criticized or others want to know how highly you think of yourself.

A VERY RICH fellow ran for governor of a southern state not too long ago. He didn't like taking directions from people. He was, after all, his own man. He had become very successful on his own, and he thought there was nothing useful anyone could teach him because he already knew everything he needed to know.

Two things came out of this belief. One, people felt that he was full of himself, disagreeable, and not someone they particularly liked or trusted. And, two, when during a debate televised statewide he didn't know the answer to how the state passed a budget, people felt like his pompous image was a phony mask covering up for the fact that he really wasn't that capable. This man didn't become governor or senator or anything else he ran for. He told people he was too capable to listen and learn. The people told him he was just incapable of listening and learning.

In studies on married couples, a significant connection is found between rigidity in one partner and discord in the relationship. Where one partner is convinced he or she is correct and therefore not open to suggestion, the length of time disagreements continue is about three times as great. (Botwin, Buss, and Shackelford 1997)

18

Don't Face Your Problems Alone

Problems can appear to be unsolvable. We are social creatures who need to discuss our problems with others, whether it be those who care about us most or those who have faced the same problems we have. When we are alone, problems fester. By sharing, we can gain perspective and find solutions.

IT IS A FAMILIAR story that the folks at Credit Counseling hear all too often. It goes like this: Sam missed a mortgage payment. Then he missed a second. Then he missed a third. Then the bank came and took his house away.

When he missed the first payment, all kinds of things could have been done. Arrangements could have been made that would have protected Sam and his house. Sam had friends who knew the rules, who could have helped. Sam didn't ask. He was embarrassed. He got himself into trouble, and he was going to get himself out of trouble.

Problem was, Sam didn't know how to get himself out of trouble. He didn't know what to do, and as days passed and his situation grew more grave, Sam only became more upset, more embarrassed. As a consequence, he isolated himself even more from his friends. Before they knew what hit Sam, he was out the door. Credit Counseling's counselors tell people, "The only thing that hiding your problems accomplishes is making sure no one helps you with them."

An experiment was conducted with a group of women having low life satisfaction. Some of the women were introduced to others who shared their situation, and some of the women were left on their own to deal with their concerns. Those who interacted with others saw a 55 percent reduction in their concerns over time, while those who were left on their own showed no improvement. (Hunter and Liao 1995)

Age Is Not to Be Feared

Older people are as happy as younger people. While they must make accommodations for age, seniors often report serene satisfaction with their life.

MR. NELSON, as he is known, is a familiar fixture in his South Florida neighborhood. You always see him in his garden or taking his daily afternoon bicycle ride. He seems to be friends with everyone and always has a story to tell when you stop to talk to him.

If you ask him, he'll tell you that he has a cherished routine that fills his day with activities he enjoys. Mr. Nelson is ninety years old.

Far from regretting his age, he revels in it. He feels the wisdom of his years, and instead of facing the responsibilities that younger people with jobs have, he has little to worry about.

When people ask him about his age, he smiles and says, "I'm old, yes, but consider the alternative."

Surveys and an analysis of previous studies show that age is simply unrelated to levels of personal happiness. (Kehn 1995)

Develop a Household Routine

We often feel overwhelmed by the chores that have to be done on a regular basis. We clean the kitchen, then the living room needs to be vacuumed, the yard needs to be mowed, and sixteen other things need to be done. Set up a reasonable schedule to do your work, and instead of facing an endless chore, you will have a list of tasks to accomplish each day. With a routine, you will not be lost in wondering what's next.

ERNIE IS A TEACHER. He often tells his students that while he loves teaching, a part of him would love to be a builder. What is so great about builders? Ernie admires the fact that builders have to do things in an orderly process. They start by laying the foundation, then they put up the walls, the roof, the floors. Not only is it orderly, it is also easy for builders to assess their progress. At any time, builders can immediately see what has been accomplished.

Ernie tells his students that when they take on tasks, especially major recurring chores like homework or housework, they need to emulate builders. We need to set an order for things that need to be done; otherwise we tend to start one job, get distracted by something else, then look around and feel like we haven't accomplished anything. When we approach tasks like a builder, we finish what we start, and every step of the way we can see that we are closer to being finished.

In studies of families, regularity in household routines improved daily personal satisfaction by about 5 percent. (Henry and Lovelace 1995)

21

Don't Be Overprotective

None of us wants our loved ones to experience any harm, but we have to let them lead their lives. Spending our time worrying and trying to prevent them from doing what they want is a real risk in itself and will keep us worrying all the time.

EVERYTHING, ABSOLUTELY everything, has a risk associated with it.

Some people become racked with fear over the possible dangers for themselves, their loved ones, and their children. Think about this for a moment: over the last seven years fear of crime has dramatically risen, while the actual crime rate has fallen.

People have become more afraid even as they have less to be worried about. The danger, as Franklin Roosevelt once suggested, is that the fear can become worse than the thing feared.

Not leaving the house or keeping the kids from playing a sport or avoiding other things because we are afraid is no solution for possible danger. It is only a different danger. While we certainly need to make sensible decisions, we need to consider the downside of avoiding the things that make life worthwhile.

Studies of thousands of parents found that there were negatives associated with being very protective, including increased time spent worrying and a generally higher level of stress. In sum, being more protective does not offer people more life satisfaction or contentment. (Voydanoff and Donnelly 1998)

22

Pay Attention. You May Have What You Want

We often forget to sit down and think about where we started and where we are now. The human tendency is to always want more. A better approach is to remember where you started and appreciate how much you have accomplished.

ARTHUR WAS a hard-charging advertising executive. After three promotions in five years, he was working longer hours than ever before. He had gotten closer and closer to the top, and he could almost taste it now. Six-day workweeks with long hours were not enough, so he brought work home with him.

When he woke up in the recovery room after a triple bypass heart operation, he began to reassess. During three weeks of recovery, his family and best friends saw more of him than they had in decades. He cherished the time.

Arthur's wife asked him if he really needed to work the schedule he had. Did they need more money? Did he really need another promotion? Arthur, challenged to actually think about his life—something he never took the time to do when he was working—realized he had more than he needed and that the opportunity to reconnect with his family was the greatest gift he could be given.

In research on highly educated professionals, almost half of the subjects could not become satisfied even as they accomplished their apparent goals because they did not recognize their accomplishments and instead created an irrational negative image of themselves. (Thurman 1981)

23

Don't Let Your Religious Beliefs Fade

Religion can show us the way in a world in which bad things happen. It can teach us that much of what we see is so complex we cannot understand why and how it occurred.

EVERYWHERE IN OUR world there is mystery. Everywhere there are questions. Religion offers answers, religion offers consistency, religion offers hope.

Doris is in her seventies and has had two heart attacks and cancer. By any normal medical calculation, she would be dead. Instead, she visits with her grandchildren and takes time to meet with medical students to discuss the importance of religious faith to her survival. Doris believes that without her religion she wouldn't have survived.

Skeptical? It's just one woman's opinion, after all.

Researchers at the Harvard Medical School, the National Institutes of Health, and countless other centers have backed up her claim. Active religious practices, their studies find, are associated with longer, healthier, and, yes, happier lives.

While doctors don't necessarily understand why this is, Father McGlone, a priest, thinks religion is important "not because we know all the answers, but because we have the best answer there is: faith."

Research on the effect of religion on life satisfaction found that regardless of what religion people affiliated themselves with, those who had strongly held spiritual beliefs were typically satisfied with life, while those who had no spiritual beliefs typically were unsatisfied. (Gerwood, LeBlanc, and Piazza 1998)

24

Do What You Say You Are Going to Do

Nothing kills progress or deadens enthusiasm more than someone who talks but never follows through. It is crucial in both your home life and your work life that you stay focused and committed to whatever you say you will do.

A USED CAR SALESMAN shows you a car. The odometer reads 07,000. The car is about five years old. You think the car has 107,000 miles on it, but the used car salesman says that it really has just 7,000 miles; it was owned by a little old lady, and she hardly ever drove it. Do you believe the salesman?

Probably you think about all the stories you've heard about dishonest people who sell cars, and you dismiss the salesman's story. Used car salesmen lack a fundamental necessity for positive communication: credibility.

We need to believe people tell the truth if we are going to interact with them, listen to them, trust them. The same rule applies in your own family settings and work settings. You cannot break your promises and expect to continue to be credible, even if you have the best intentions.

It's important to remember, credibility is like the bottom of a ship. If it has holes, it doesn't matter whether they are big or little—they all matter.

The difference between those who have happy personal relationships and those who have unhappy personal relationships is not the amount of conflicts they have. Indeed, each group has a similar number of conflicts. Instead, it is a greater commitment to following through on agreed-upon changes that contributes to the success of relationships and the 23 percent greater happiness of the individuals involved. (Turner 1994)

25

Don't Be Aggressive with Your Friends and Family

Even if you are right, there is nothing to be gained from letting yourself become adversarial with your loved ones. Remember how much more important these people are to you than is the issue you are talking about.

IT WOULD BE great to always be right, wouldn't it?

Adam is always right. At least, he thinks so. Whether it's a matter of a trivia question or the best way to hang wallpaper, Adam knows the answer. When his family challenges him on some point, any point, Adam launches an inquest. He asks people to tell him why they disagree, and then he tries to catch them in an inconsistency. His follow-up questions are like those used by a lawyer trying to get an unreliable witness to admit his faults.

Adam almost always wins. He almost always gets a concession from his witness. The problem is, Adam's witness is not a criminal in a courtroom but a friend or loved one who holds a different opinion. Some of his friends have concluded it's just not worth disagreeing with Adam, and others have concluded it's not even worth talking to Adam, since you never know when a topic will lead to a controversy. Adam wins all the little battles, but he loses the metaphorical war. He loses the opportunity to spend enjoyable time with those he cares about.

Prevalent criticism within relationships reduces happiness up to one-third. (O'Connor 1995)

26

Root for the Home Team

Living with the ups and downs of your area's favorite sports team will help you feel a part of the community and show you how much you have in common with your neighbors.

PEOPLE IN SOUTHERN Indiana root for the Indiana University basketball team. Almost everybody roots for the Hoosiers. What's neat about that is that people from all walks of life immediately have something in common. The mechanic and the doctor, the schoolteacher and the chef, the janitor and the mayor may not have a lot of similar interests, but they can all discuss Indiana's season.

The team gives the community the chance not only to hold a common interest but also to come together on game day. And when the team plays away games, it's not unusual to see house after house tuned to the game. Walk down the street and you'll hear conversations about the team and immediately feel that you are a part of the community, that something binds you and your neighbors and the rest of the city together.

Stanley, a lifelong Indiana fan, planned his wedding around the Indiana basketball schedule. His wife-to-be didn't mind, though; they had met at an Indiana game. And other than getting married at halftime, she wouldn't have had it any other way.

Rooting for a local sports team was found to have positive effects by providing a common interest with others in the community and increasing happiness by 4 percent. (Shank and Beasley 1998)

Don't Confuse Stuff with Success

Y̶ou are neither a better nor worse person for the kind of car you drive, the size of your home, or the performance of your mutual funds. Remember what really matters in your life.

IMAGINE FOR A MOMENT that today was your last day on Earth. Now, make a list for yourself of all the things that you feel you have accomplished, all the things you are proud of, and all the things that make you happy.

Is your car on the list? Your television? Your stereo? Is your salary on the list? No. What's on the list are the fundamental elements of a satisfied life—your relationship with friends and family, the contribution you have made to others' lives, the celebrated events of your life. Those are the building blocks of your list.

Many of us live day to day as if the opposite were true. Instead of appreciating what is truly important and making that our priority, we collect things and indicators of success without questioning just what success really means.

In a study using surveys and daily observation, the availability of material resources was nine times less important to happiness than the availability of "personal" resources such as friends and family. (Diener and Fujita 1995)

Every Relationship Is Different

If you've been disappointed by strained relations with a friend or loved one, you must realize that each relationship is unique. Don't let tension with one person convince you that you lack the ability to be a good friend or a loving family member.

JANE HAS A GOOD relationship with her parents and her brother. With her sister, though, she has never really gotten along. She is frustrated by this, always questioning why she can't duplicate the easy times she has with her parents and her brother. What's wrong with me? Jane asks herself. But what Jane does that makes her parents so happy and her brother so happy has the opposite effect on her sister. What is funny and charming to the rest of her family is seen as phony by her sister. To change to please her sister, though, would not only be difficult, it would alter the positive relationships Jane has.

Why can't we take our positive relationships that we enjoy with some people and duplicate them with everyone we know? The answer, say psychologists at Canada's McGill University, is that "people are too complex, they have too many facets" to be expected to react the same way as each other.

What can we do? We need to accept that our getting along with most but not all our loved ones is not a flaw but a reality. The university researchers explain, "More satisfied people do not have happy relationships with everyone. They appreciate their happy relationships and accept their imperfect relationships."

Researchers found there were no differences in overall happiness between those who mainly relied upon friends for companionship and those who mainly relied upon family. People have the capacity to create happiness from the relationships available to them and do not need all their relationships to fit an ideal image. (Takahashi, Tamura, and Tokoro 1997)

29

Don't Think "What If ...?"

S pending your time imagining what would have been if you could have changed some little thing, some little decision in your life, is counterproductive and leaves you unhappy. Think about how you can improve for the future, but don't waste your present thinking about how you could have changed the past.

WE COULD TRACE our current position to every decision we have ever made. Where you sat in kindergarten influenced who your friends were, which influenced what your interests were, which influenced how you did in school, and so forth.

We could ponder these things endlessly, but it wouldn't get us any-where. Take a wrong turn on your way somewhere, and it won't pay to pull over and question why or how you took the wrong turn. What you need to do is think about how you can get from where you are to where you want to be.

The same applies to your life: don't wallow in disappointment over how you got to where you are. Think about what you need to do to get where you want to be.

Research on athletes who came close but lost in Olympic finals finds that those who spend the least time on counterfactual thought—thinking about how things might have ended differently—are the most satisfied with their experience. (Gilovich and Medvec 1995)

30

Volunteer

Every community has countless opportunities for giving of yourself. Be a reading tutor. Give your time to help the local charity thrift store. Anything you can do will not only help the world, it will also help you. Volunteers feel good about themselves. They have a sense of purpose, feel appreciated, and are less likely to be bored in their lives. Volunteers experience rewards that cannot be attained in any other way. Even if you don't have a lot of time or skills, find an hour a month and give yourself to a good cause.

BESSIE IS A WIDOW in her seventies. She found herself with time on her hands and a desire to do something useful with it. She wanted something that would make her want to get up in the morning with a smile on her face.

Bessie found out about a foster grandparent program run out of a Buffalo area community center. The program uses senior citizens to offer companionship to disabled children during the day.

Bessie signed up and now spends a couple of hours a day playing, reading, talking, and sitting with the children.

One of Bessie's friends, who also volunteers in the same program, says that the foster grandparents give the children "love and attention," and in return they are rewarded by getting a chance to see "the beauty in every one of these children."

Bessie says the volunteer work "gives me the feeling that I am doing something good. I'm helping the children, the parents, and myself. Everybody wins, but I always feel I win the most."

An analysis of volumes of previous research on the subject shows a strong consensus that volunteering contributes to happiness by decreasing boredom and creating an increased sense of purpose in life. Volunteers, on average, are twice as likely to feel happy with themselves as nonvolunteers. (Crist-Houran 1996)

31

If You Can't Reach Your Goals, Your Goals Will Hurt You

People who cannot attain their goals become consumed with disappointment. You must let your goals evolve with your life circumstances. Update your goals over time as you consider your changing priorities and resources.

UNIVERSITY OF MICHIGAN psychologists have found great evidence that while goals are important, goals can do us a great disservice if they are not flexible. Here's a typical story.

Jimmy proposed to his girlfriend when he was only eighteen. She accepted, and they were married a year later. At the time, Jimmy promised that he would buy them a house before he turned twenty-four. Jimmy took the first in a series of jobs. None of them paid very well. Jimmy and his bride lived in a modest but comfortable apartment. As the clock ticked on, though, Jimmy saved as much as he could, got down-payment money from his parents, and eked out a mortgage approval. Jimmy and his wife moved in, and then they celebrated. The payments were more than he could afford, though.

Soon he took on a second job. It wasn't enough.

Jimmy took another part-time job, his third.

He worked himself sick and over time began to resent both the house and the wife that he had promised it to.

Instead of continuing a life he found satisfying and continuing to save for a house someday, Jimmy rushed the process to meet his declared goal. He let a rigid goal change his life, which was the same as letting a rigid goal harm his life.

If a person's goals are incongruent with his or her abilities, then the goals will contribute to disappointment and disagreeableness, and will quadruple the likelihood of being dissatisfied. (Pavot, Fujita, and Diener 1997)

Exercise

P eople who exercise, whether that involves an intense workout or just a regular long walk, feel healthier, feel better about themselves, and enjoy life more.

A PROMINENT EXECUTIVE used to say, "Whenever the thought occurs to me that maybe I should exercise, I lie down until the thought passes."

He said this a lot, and, not surprisingly, his philosophy led him directly to a lack of energy and, soon, to health problems.

His doctors impressed on him the necessity of changing his lifestyle, and the executive gave it a try. To his surprise, he found he actually enjoyed exercising. It was a chance to spend some time every day, without any worries or concerns, doing something positive. And instead of making him tired, exercise actually increased his energy.

What's his philosophy now? "I enjoy exercise so much, I can hardly put it into words."

Research on physical activity finds that exercise increases self-confidence, which in turn strengthens self-evaluations. Regular exercise, including brisk walks, directly increases happiness 12 percent, and can indirectly make a dramatic contribution to improving self-image. (Fontane 1996)

Little Things Have Big Meanings

Tiny things—the tone of your voice, the exact words you use as you go through otherwise ordinary events—communicate volumes.

DO LITTLE THINGS, like a slight change in your facial expression, really matter?

Humans don't swell up like blowfish or change colors like chameleons. Our reactions are seen in more subtle expressions, tones of voice, and body language.

Consider this: recognizing someone's facial expression takes less than one-sixth of a second. We can process expressions from as far as 100 yards away. How can we do this? We pay attention. Humans are attuned to facial expressions as an indicator of what their companions are thinking. Because we think facial expressions are important, we pay attention to them. Because we pay attention to facial expressions, we react to them. Because we react, facial expressions become important to our communication.

The next time someone asks you if you like the dinner they made, and you say "It's good," remember the other person is paying attention not only to what you say, but also to other messages you might be communicating.

Married couples who display sensitivity in communication—who recognize the power of subtle changes in demeanor—rate their satisfaction 17 percent higher than couples who do not. (Notarius 1996)

It's Not What Happened, It's How You Think About What Happened

There is no objective way to tell you if you have had a good life, a good day, or a good hour. Your life is a success based only upon your judgment.

A STUDY WAS done recently in which people on opposite sides of an issue were given the same newspaper article to read. The people were asked to read the article carefully and to offer their reaction. On average, people said they thought the article was biased—against their own position. That is, people on both sides of the issue thought the exact same article was biased against their side. The article could not possibly have been biased against both sides of the issue. Obviously, it wasn't the content of the article that drove the reaction, but the perspective of the readers. Life events have the same effect. The same event can be seen positively, or it can be seen negatively. It depends upon your perspective.

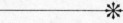

Knowing whether someone has recently suffered a personal setback or personal triumph is not as good a predictor of how satisfied they are with their lives as is knowing how they perceive the causes and consequences of those events. (Staats, Armstrong-Stassen, and Partillo 1995)

Develop Some Common Interests
with Loved Ones

Common interests can make it more fun to be around your family and friends. They can allow you to see that your bonds are much deeper than just circumstance.

EVERY MEMBER of Tom's family loves jumping out of planes. "It may be strange to some people, but it's really a nice way to spend the day together with your family," explained Tom.

Tom and his son first tried skydiving together, and they enjoyed it so much they decided to take lessons together so they could learn to jump without a guide.

Soon Tom's wife and their daughter were joining them—with the whole family jumping out of planes together.

On a typical weekend, the family spends hours together traveling to and from the jump site, and they might jump out of their plane four or five times.

Tom's family loves the fun of their hobby, and they love the chance it gives them to spend time together. Tom and his wife even renewed their wedding vows at 4,000 feet, before jumping out of the plane together, as their children and guests looked on.

Each common interest between people in a relationship increases the likelihood of a lasting relationship and results in an increase in life satisfaction of about 2 percent. (Chand 1990)

Laugh

Don't spend your time evaluating humor, asking yourself, "Is it really funny?" or "Do others think it's funny?" Just react and enjoy it.

A GROUP CALLED the American Association for Therapy and Humor believes that one of the things too often missing from our days is a good laugh.

The message is being heard by an increasing number of business consultants, who find that a little laughter makes for a better employee.

Businesses across the country have Dress Like Elvis Days, clown squads that roam the halls sharing mirth, and silly contests like seeing who can throw a paper airplane the farthest.

Why?

Shaking us out of our routine increases creativity, productivity, and job satisfaction.

But whether at work or at home, the Therapy and Humor group says, "Happiness is a laughing matter."

In studies of hundreds of adults, happiness was found to be related to humor. The ability to laugh, whether at life itself or at a good joke, is a source of life satisfaction. Indeed, those who enjoy silly humor are one-third more likely to feel happy. (Solomon 1996)

Don't Let Your Entire Life Hinge on One Element

Your life is made up of many different facets. Don't focus on one aspect of your life so much that you can't experience pleasure if that one area is unsettled. It can become all you think about, and it can deaden your enjoyment of everything else—things you would otherwise love.

WOULD YOU INVEST every dollar you had in the stock of one company?

Of course not. Every expert you could possibly consult would tell you to invest by diversifying. You shouldn't place all your hopes on one company or even one kind of company. Instead, you should intelligently pursue a variety of investments, with no one central investment capable of ruining your savings.

The same applies to living your life: you should diversify your hopes.

Don't pin all your hopes on getting a promotion and wind up ruining what could have been a satisfying home life by lack of progress in the office.

Don't define your life based on having a perfect relationship with one family member and wind up feeling devastated by a strained relationship.

Build your hopes around the many things that are important to you, and allow yourself to benefit from the different things that contribute to your life, rather than allowing yourself to be devastated by a single bump in the road.

In an experiment in which subjects were asked to discuss the life satisfaction of others, subjects tended to calculate likelihood of happiness on an "averaging" scale. That is, happiness was associated with people whose lives were generally positive in multiple areas that mattered to them. (Bhargava 1995)

38

Share of Yourself

D on't hold inside your feelings, your thoughts, your hopes. Share them with your friends and family. People who hold things inside tend to feel isolated, believing that others do not understand them. Those who share feel both supported and more content, even if events do not go exactly as they wish.

ROSE HAS BEEN an artist for many years. In her spare time she would paint beautiful watercolor landscapes. From time to time, she would display her work in the local art show or have some of her pieces shown in a small art shop and gallery. Whenever her family asked her about her art, their question was either "Did you sell anything?" or "How much did you make?" Rose felt like this wonderful form of expression, this way of being herself that was so important to her, was completely misunderstood. She wasn't trying to make money, she didn't care if it sold. She painted for herself, not for profit. Every time she was asked whether she made any money, she would churn inside.

Why don't they understand me? Rose wondered. Why do these people, who should be so close to me, seem so distant and removed? These thoughts grew inside of her and caused her to become less comfortable around her family. Then Rose realized that her family couldn't read her mind and that part of the reason they didn't understand her was that she hadn't explained what was really important to her.

Individuals who tend to be socially open rate their overall life satisfaction 24 percent higher than individuals who do not. (Finch, Barrera, Okun, Bryant, Pool, and Snow-Turek 1997)

39

Busy Is Better Than Bored

F ind something to do, because the feeling that we have too much to do is much more pleasing than the feeling that we have nothing to do.

A PHILOSOPHER ONCE noted that people long for immortality but run out of things to do on a rainy afternoon. If we planned out our time in long chunks, say twenty years, we would never consider penciling in five or ten of those years for wasting time. Yet during the average day, we often let a few hours slip away. Time is a strange commodity, because we seem to have so much of it, until the moment we have none at all. We often complain about having too much to do. Yet having too much to do is a positive problem of abundance, while having too little to do is a negative problem of shortage.

Metro Plastics Technology in Indiana tested out this principle by cutting the length of the workweek for its employees from forty hours to thirty hours. And do you know what happened after the switch? The quality of the company's products improved, and the company actually made more money. Management found that giving workers more to do in less time made the workers more efficient, energetic, and enthusiastic and gave workers more free time outside of the workplace.

In studies of college students, those with more demanding schedules were 15 percent more satisfied with life. Despite the more demanding schedules, the individuals studied did not experience any more stress than those with less to do. (Bailey and Miller 1998)

40

Satisfaction Is Relative

Your happiness is relative to a scale you yourself have created. If you measure your satisfaction right now against the two or three greatest moments in your life, you will often be unhappy because those moments can't be duplicated. If you measure today's satisfaction against some tough days you've had, you have all the reason in the world to appreciate this moment.

IS BOBBY A GOOD student? Well, are you comparing him to his classmates or to Einstein? Is Harrison Ford a good actor? Well, are you comparing him to Keanu Reeves or to Robert De Niro? Was today a good day? Well, are you comparing it to graduations, weddings, and celebrations, or to your typical Tuesday? We need to consider things in a realistic perspective.

Anthropologists at Rutgers University are finding that one of the most significant determinants of people's enjoyment of work is their feelings about their home life. Many people are finding their work more tolerable because their family situations have become more stressful.

The Rutgers team finds that people are clinging to the order and friendship available in the workplace and that the often hectic, pressure-filled home life suffers by comparison.

The sad reality, of course, is that your home life cannot duplicate those aspects of the workplace and shouldn't be expected to. Jobs should be compared to other jobs but not to the home, where everything is both more complex, and offers more potential rewards.

A good day on the job should be thought of relative to other days on the job. A good day at home should be thought of relative to other days at home.

Not surprisingly, surveys find that happy people tend to have more positive experiences than unhappy people. What is striking is that, objectively, their lives aren't really much different. Studies find that happy people experience much the same range of events as unhappy people. The real difference is in what they define as positive and negative. Happy people are those who use a lower threshold in order to label an event positive. (Parducci 1995)

Learn to Use a Computer

Whether they are eight or ninety-eight, people who use computers experience the wonders of technology and of the world.

COMPUTERS CAN HELP bring people together, and nowhere is that more important than for people who are constantly being moved apart. For example, computers allow access to e-mail, and these instant messages are becoming crucial to military families, who often have to live apart from one another and who even more regularly must settle in new communities apart from their friends.

Melody, a fifth-grader whose father is in the army, has recently lived in Kentucky, Illinois, Texas, and Colorado. While she finds it hard to always move away and sometimes watch friends move away, her computer lets her stay in touch with friends who are scattered across the country.

The army has found that computers have made military relocations a little bit easier for the entire family because they can use the computer to find out about their new home and to stay in touch with friends they are leaving behind.

In a study of senior citizens introduced to personal computers, self-esteem and life satisfaction were found to improve by about 5 percent as a result of computer use. (Sherer 1996)

Try to Think Less About the People and Things That Bother You

There are an infinite number of things you could spend your time thinking about, but many of us concentrate great attention on those things that we find most upsetting. Don't ignore what bothers you, but don't focus on it to the exclusion of the things you enjoy.

RALPH OWNS the corner lot on a crowded Chicago block. He counts his immediate neighbors as friends. One of his neighbors is also his family doctor.

The problem is access to backyards. The houses are right on top of each other, and the only way any of his neighbors can drive to their backyards is through Ralph's yard. But Ralph often parks his car in his yard, which blocks the path of any of his neighbors to their yards. They can walk to their yards, they just can't drive there.

Do they really need to drive to their backyards? Not very often, but the fact that they couldn't because Ralph's car was in the way irritated some of them.

Ralph's neighbors researched the city ordinances and found an 1892 rule that appeared to grant them access to Ralph's yard to get to their own. Ralph said the 1892 rule gives them the right to walk through his backyard, not drive through it.

These friends and neighbors soon became neither, for they got together—including the family doctor—and sued Ralph for auto access to their backyards. Relationships deteriorated, all because no one was prepared to sacrifice something that wasn't really important for the sake of peace and friendship.

Those who regularly ruminate over negative subjects and unhappiness are 70 percent less likely to feel content than those who do not. (Scott and McIntosh 1999)

43

Keep Your Family Close

A s family members scatter across the country, it becomes easy to forget to include them in your thoughts and in your time. Keep up the contact, share with your family the news of your life. They want to know, and you will feel better if your bond is maintained.

TWO DECADES AGO, Sally moved away from her family's home to go to college. Her mother recalls the time sadly: "It was horrible. I wanted her to pursue her dreams, but I didn't want to lose her. I felt that she wanted to abandon me, that she wanted to be gone."

Sally took her mother's reaction as a sign of her mother's insecurity instead of her love, and they grew apart. "She'd ask me why I'd gone so far away. I didn't process it. I felt it was her problem."

Sally's career kept her geographically distant from her family. Over time, Sally's mother showed less and less concern for Sally's decisions. Sally worried that her mother did not care, and their relationship remained as distant as their locations.

Then, Sally realized that beneath the initial concern and her mother's more recent reaction, was the same thing: love.

Geography now is no longer a barrier. Sally and her mother communicate regularly, and Sally cherishes the opportunity to visit her hometown. Sally cautions that both those who leave and those who stay have to remember that being apart does not have to mean being distant from each other.

Studies that examine the importance of family to senior citizens as compared to adults not yet entering middle age show family relationships to be an equally crucial component of life satisfaction for both age groups. (O'Connor 1995)

44

Eat Some Fruit Every Day

Fruit eaters feel good about what they eat, are less interested in eating junk food, and ultimately feel better about themselves.

HAVE YOU NOTICED that even though there are magazines that you would never buy and never go out of your way to read, you will pick them up when you're stuck in a waiting room? Out of desperation and convenience, we accept things that do not appeal to us. The same applies to what we eat. We're in a hurry, and we don't want to spend a lot of energy or time on food. Often it's like we're in that waiting room, going for the first food we see.

Keep fruit in the house, and eat it as a snack. It's easy, it's cheap, it requires no preparation time, and it's great for you. Study after study shows the physical benefits of eating fruit, and now we know it has emotional benefits as well. Our bodies crave sweet tastes, which originally was an evolutionary advantage, for it led early humans to consume more fruit. Only in modern times, when sugary sweets have become available to us, has our taste for sweets had negative consequences.

Eating fruit is associated with a number of positive life habits that contribute to both health and happiness, and eating more fruit is associated with an 11 percent higher likelihood of feeling capable and satisfied. (Heatey and Thombs 1997)

Enjoy What You Have

People who are satisfied appreciate what they have in life and don't worry about how it compares to what others have. Valuing what you have over what you do not or cannot have leads to greater happiness.

FOUR-YEAR-OLD Alice runs to the Christmas tree and sees wonderful presents beneath it. No doubt she has received fewer presents than some of her friends, and probably she has not received some of the things she most wanted. But at that moment, she doesn't stop to think why aren't there more presents or to wonder what she may have asked for that she didn't get. Instead, she marvels at the treasures before her.

When we think about our lives, too often we think about what we don't have and what we didn't get. But such a focus denies us pleasure. You wouldn't sit next to the Christmas tree and remind Alice that there were presents she didn't receive. Why remind yourself of the things in life you don't have when you could remind yourself of what you do have?

People who have the most are only as likely to be happy as those who have the least. People who like what they have, however, are twice as likely to be happy as those who actually have the most. (Sirgy, Cole, Kosenko, and Meadow 1995)

Think in Concrete Terms

We need to be able to measure our progress, to know that things are improving. You can't accomplish an abstract goal, because you'll never be sure if you're finished or not.

I WANT TO BE a better worker. I want to be a better parent. I want to be a better friend. Many of us have these kinds of hopes—vague hopes. The problem with these kinds of ideas is that they are not specific. They include no step-by-step directions and no outcomes. You want to be a better worker. Well, what does that mean? How does someone do that? How will you know if you've succeeded or not?

StarQuest is a consulting firm in Houston that teaches goal setting—specifically, how to make your goals clear and direct. They advise you to think about what you care about, and then think about what you can actually do to accomplish that.

You might set as your goals: I want to finish this weekly report an hour faster; I want to make this task 5 percent cheaper; I want to have dinner with my family one more night per week; I want to make it to all my daughter's soccer games. Here your goals come with built-in directions. These are goals that you can work toward and successfully complete. Completing any goal we set for ourselves improves our confidence and satisfaction and steadies us for the future.

Perceptions that life is meaningful, and therefore worthwhile, increase 16 percent with concrete thinking. (Lindeman and Verkasalo 1996)

Be Socially Supportive

Take the time to help, comfort, or just be with those you care about when they are in need. You will feel good about your efforts, and it will bring you an even closer relationship.

SARAH WASN'T SURE she could make it through all her high school courses, then to college, on her way to a goal of becoming a teacher. Often it took her longer than any of her classmates to finish readings and assignments, and every step along the way was arduous.

Her friends spent many days helping Sarah, especially with her readings.

On graduation night Sarah, soon bound for an Ivy League school, thanked those friends for their help, faith, and support. She spoke to her classmates as the first blind valedictorian in school history.

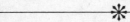

The need for support or the number of problems individuals face is a less strong predictor of their happiness than the amount of support available to them. (Jou and Fukada 1997)

Don't Blame Yourself

When things go poorly, we sometimes start a list of ways we failed, ways we caused the problem. This kind of thinking not only can upset us, it also can keep us from being able to function. The truth is that any situation is the result of some things that are in your control and some things that are out of your control. Don't delude yourself into thinking a bad situation is completely of your making. Remember, it makes more sense to deal with outcomes than with fault.

COMPANY IS COMING, and the dishwasher is spouting water. The flood is spreading across the kitchen floor, heading for the living room. You think to yourself, Why did I have to do the dishes right now? Or, If I had washed the dishes by hand, this wouldn't be happening. If I had waited to use the dishwasher tomorrow, it wouldn't be ruining my night now. It's obvious, if only I had sense enough to see the facts. Why did I even buy this dishwasher? I bet if I had gone with a different model, it wouldn't be flooding my kitchen right now!

When things go wrong we look to lay blame, and often we look in the mirror. Psychologists at the National Institute of Mental Health find that many of us fall victim to the "everything is my fault" approach to life.

Two things we often overlook is how little we directly control a situation and how little value there is in spending our time blaming ourselves. These thoughts do not fix the problem. These thoughts do not make anything better. Blame is about the past; a plan of action to fix a problem is about the future.

Happiness does not depend on how many bad things happen to an individual. What is more important is whether an individual tends to make negative conclusions about him- or herself when negative events occur. Individuals who think of themselves as the cause of negative events are 43 percent less likely to be satisfied than individuals who do not. (Panos 1997)

Be a Peacemaker

If your friends or family members are upset with one another, you will feel their unhappiness. Try to be the voice of reason and reconciliation.

NELLIE AND CINDY are sisters from northern California. They were close all their lives, and they even decided to move in together to share Nellie's house.

And then the phone bill came.

Nellie received what she called the biggest phone bill of her life and immediately confronted her sister. Cindy looked at the bill and said that most of the calls weren't hers; they must have been placed by Nellie.

Words escalated, until the tension between the sisters completely eclipsed their familial bonds. The rest of their family members felt uncomfortable in their presence and began to avoid them rather than trying to help them through the difficulty.

With no compromise in sight, Nellie sued her own sister in small claims court. The family was exasperated with the both of them.

And even while Nellie won the case, she lost her sister.

The passive avoidance of problems between loved ones reduces contentment by 15 percent. To keep in contact and maintain happiness, difficulties must be faced rather than avoided. (Simpson 1990)

Cherish Animals

A nimals have so much to teach us about love. The closer we get to animals, the more joy they give us.

GINA RUNS a nursing home. She has tried all kinds of things to brighten the days for her senior citizens. What works better than anything else is dogs.

The local animal shelter brings in a vanload of small dogs every Thursday afternoon, and the seniors immediately smile. The dogs offer unconditional love, and the residents of the nursing home, who often feel isolated and withdrawn, take that love and are energized by it. Softened by the love, they return it right back to their furry friends.

"You just have to watch one of these dogs put his head under a listless hand, demanding to be petted, or rest his chin on a patient's chest and stare lovingly into their eyes, or see someone who wouldn't get out of bed offer to hold the leash and take a dog for a walk down the hall" to see how much dogs can help, according to one volunteer. "You can actually see dogs bring people out of themselves and help them forget their troubles. Blank faces come alive, and eyes uncloud."

Interaction with animals supplies us with both immediate joy and long-term positive feelings, and contributes strongly to our happiness. Those with a loved pet are 22 percent more likely to feel satisfied than those without. (Barofsky and Rowan 1998)

51

Make Your Work a Calling

If you see your work as only a job, then it's dragging you away from what you really want to be doing. If you see it as a calling, then it is no longer a toiling sacrifice. Instead, it becomes an expression of you, a part of you.

VICTOR IS A MOTORMAN for the Chicago Transit Authority. Five days a week he's running an elevated train on the Red Line. Victor stands out in the minds of the people who ride his train because of a notable and unusual trait: he loves his job.

"Thank you for riding with me this evening on Electric Avenue. Don't lean against the doors, I don't want to lose you," he tells passengers over the intercom as the train departs.

As the train makes its way north, Victor points out notable sites, including which connecting buses are waiting in the street below.

People compliment him all the time, telling the city he's the best motorman in Chicago.

Victor admits, "Our equipment may be junky, but for $1.50 I want to give a Lincoln Town Car ride."

Why does Victor have such a positive approach to his job? "My father is a retired motorman, and one day he took me to work with him and I was so impressed looking out that window," he says, speaking of the city skyline. "Ever since I was five years old, I knew I wanted to run the trains."

In research on working women, researchers found that even for those working in the same kinds of jobs, work was alternatively viewed either as a series of hassles or as a positive experience in which the women were in control of their lives. Among those who felt in control, life satisfaction was 28 percent higher than among those who did not. (Thakar and Misra 1995)

Never Trade Your Morals for Your Goals

People who compromise what they believe in to satisfy their goals wind up dissatisfied with their accomplishments. If you do not believe yourself to be moral, satisfaction is unattainable.

A FEW YEARS back, a student at Yale was expelled. His transgression was that he had faked all the documents in his application: his grades, his letters of recommendation, his activities. His fake application looked so good that Yale admitted him.

The student actually did well in his classes and was nearing graduation.

How did he get caught? He confessed. He simply could not keep quiet about his fake application, even though his real course work was about to get him a degree. The fact that his achievement would always be predicated on a lie made it no achievement at all.

Being happy and being moral buttress each other. People who feel they lack morals report they are half as likely to feel happy compared to those who feel they are moral. (Garrett 1996)

Don't Pretend to Ignore Things Your Loved Ones Do That Bother You

In the name of being agreeable, some people try to avoid areas that might cause dissension. But with our loved ones, this strategy sometimes makes us uncomfortable. We can feel unappreciated because we have made a sacrifice but nobody thanks us for it. Sometimes we feel angry because this problem doesn't go away. Raise the subject of your disagreement, but do so lovingly and constructively, not with anger or aggression.

MARY IS A HAIRDRESSER. Her sister Kim is a banker. Normally, this is of little importance to Mary. But Mary's mother introduces her daughters to friends this way: "Mary's a hairdresser. Her sister's a banker, though." Inside it burns Mary every time. Why does her mother have to focus on her daughters' occupations and then say it in a way that makes it sound like she's disappointed in Mary's work?

Inevitably, when Mary visits her mother, her mother complains that Mary is unfriendly or "too down." She never considers that it is her own comments that put Mary in that state.

Mary finally explained how her mother's words felt to her, and her mother said she had no idea. She was proud of both of her daughters, and she didn't intend to make it seem that her daughters' occupations were what mattered to her.

In relationships, those who feel they can freely communicate their concerns and needs to their partner are 40 percent more likely to feel satisfied than those who do not. (Ferroni and Taffe 1997)

Get a Good Night's Sleep

Don't skimp on sleep. A full night's rest is fuel for the following day. Rested people feel they work better and are more comfortable when the day is over.

AN INTERESTING THING happened on Tuesday mornings in the fall of 1998. A study found that workers in the Northeast were 3 percent more productive than they had been on Tuesdays the autumn before.

What changed? Monday night football came on an hour earlier in 1998, and more men got a decent night's sleep as a result. Instead of games lasting past midnight, in 1998 games tended to end before 11:30 PM.

Sleep is such an easy thing to trade away to TV, to work, to anything. Sleep seems like the bottomless bank account we can never overdraw. But a good night's sleep pays dividends in every aspect of our lives.

Quality and quantity of sleep contribute to health, well-being, and a positive outlook. For those who sleep less than eight hours, every hour of sleep sacrificed results in an 8 percent less positive feeling about their day. (Pilcher and Ott 1998)

Buy What You Like

Don't accumulate possessions for the sake of having a lot of stuff. On the other hand, don't deny yourself something that you really want or need. If you buy things that are important to you, you can appreciate them every day and won't feel the need to fill your home with every item at the mall.

IN A SINGLE YEAR, Americans buy over 17 billion articles of clothing. Americans buy so much new clothing that every year we give over 200 million pounds of clothing away to the Salvation Army alone. Americans buy so much new clothing, and so quickly discard anything that is worn, that the federal government has reclassified sewing machines' place in economic growth measurements from the "apparel and upkeep" category to the "recreation" category.

Many of us accumulate so far beyond our needs that we cannot use nearly all of what we have. In those cases, we are spending more, but getting less, because the things we buy don't really serve our needs or purposes.

Other people go to the opposite extreme. Don't put off buying items that would have value to you every day merely to demonstrate your frugality, since the purpose of saving is to allow you to buy what you need.

Anticipating and accumulating consumer goods can contribute to a sense of personal well-being; however, placing too much emphasis on material goods has a diminishing effect on happiness. (Oropesa 1995)

Accomplish Something Every Day

Sometimes days fly by without anything standing out in your mind, without any tangible improvement. Every day make sure, no matter how small the effort, that you do something to make your dreams come true.

WE'VE ALL HEARD the proverb "A journey of a thousand miles begins with a single step." But that same journey is vastly easier to make if the scenery changes.

If you keep moving and see different surroundings, you know you are making progress. If you can't see the progress you are making, if every step seems to leave you in the same place, then you will have trouble believing that you are moving forward.

Every day in your life you have to see the progress. Ask yourself, What did I accomplish today? If you have an answer, if you can see the progress you have made in your journey, then you have had a valuable day, a good day.

In research on hundreds of college students, individuals were found to be happiest when they felt they were moving closer to achieving their goals. Students who could not see progress were three times less likely to feel satisfied than students who could. (McGregor and Little 1998)

Be Flexible

When we want to be with friends and family, often we want it to be on our terms. If everybody approaches relationships this way, no one will be happy. Instead of thinking only about what you want, think about what the others want too, and consider why it is important to spend time together. Accept that there are always differences between people and that if you are flexible you will enjoy your time with them more and feel closer to them.

THREE SISTERS, Donna, Marie, and April, all want to hold the family's Christmas celebration at their house. For years, they took turns, rotating to all three houses every three years. Then Donna had a child and wanted to have the family over to her house every year. She wanted her son to be able to wake up and see the tree and spend the whole day at home. Marie didn't think that was fair. She wanted things done the same as they had always been done. Marie became uncomfortable at Donna's house, and Donna became uncomfortable at Marie's. April was left in the uncomfortable position of not being able to do anything except sacrifice her own turn.

Ultimately, the conflict existed because the sisters wanted to be together as a family. However, their desire to be together on their own terms kept them from being peacefully together. It is far better to be flexible enough to sacrifice what's personally ideal to have something acceptable, than to sacrifice the acceptable to have nothing.

Nearly all individuals report significant changes in their lives and in their values over the course of time. Those who viewed these changes as inevitable and remained open to the possibility that changes would be positive were 35 percent more likely to be satisfied with their lives than those who did not. (Minetti 1997)

Events Are Temporary

Bad things happen, but usually we do not feel their effects on us forever. It's really true that time heals wounds. Your disappointments are important and serious, but your distress will pass and your life will take you in new directions. Give yourself some time.

THE DAY AFTER Dan lost his election to be mayor of his hometown, he felt like a load of bricks had dropped on him. He felt that he was a failure.

Almost thirty years later, Dan was asked about the things that defined him. Was the disappointment that had once sickened him first in his mind? No. His relationship with his wife, his life as a father, his commitment to political progress—these were the things he mentioned. Did he feel like a failure? Not at all. "Life is not wins and losses; it's how you live every day."

Studies of thousands of Americans show that happy people are not immune to negative events. Instead, they are characterized by the ability to think about other things in the aftermath of negative events. (Bless, Clore, Schwarz, and Golisano 1996)

Be Your Own Fan

We need self-reinforcement, a belief in ourselves that is strong and unwavering. Be ready to pick yourself up when you are feeling down.

THE YOUNG MAN walked up to his high school gym. A paper tacked to the wall listed the players who had made the varsity team.

Fifteen-year-old Michael Jordan looked up and down the list. He could not find his name. Michael Jordan had not made the team.

Michael Jordan is considered by most experts to be the best basketball player ever. But he had to believe in himself to get there. By the time many basketball players reach the tenth grade, they are receiving hundreds of letters from college coaches seeking to recruit them into their programs. Michael Jordan didn't receive a single letter, because Michael Jordan didn't make the team.

Michael Jordan didn't give up. He believed in himself and in his ability, and he practiced and practiced. The next year he made the team. And he became its star.

Rejection spells failure only if you do not believe in yourself. For those who believe, it is only a challenge.

The tendency to reinforce one's own self-confidence improves life satisfaction by about 20 percent for both men and women. (Seybolt and Wagner 1997)

60

Join a Group

Take an inventory of your interests. Chances are there is a group in your area dedicated to your special interest. People in groups develop positive personal relationships that tend to make them feel more comfortable around others, less lonely, and more in control of events.

BOB IS AN old-fashioned guy whose hobby is woodworking. Bob, who lives in rural Iowa, had retired and was looking for people who shared his interest.

He found himself involved with a woodworking group where he could pick up tips, exchange ideas, and correspond with people who shared his interest. Soon Bob was receiving messages from people all over the country who wanted to discuss their hobby, and he made a number of friendships.

When Bob's wife became seriously ill, he told his woodworking friends that he would be busy caring for his wife. Woodworking friends Bob had corresponded with were saddened and began discussing a project to make a get-well gift for Bob and his wife. Eventually twelve different people from across the country, including a policeman, a lawyer, an engineer, and a janitor, started working on pieces of a bookshelf.

The finished project was assembled by one of the group's members, and it was sent to Bob in Iowa.

Bob was touched by the gift. He could not believe the goodwill of his fellow woodworkers, and he was grateful that he had been a part of such a wonderful group.

Group membership tends to make people feel more connected to each other and increases personal confidence and satisfaction by 7 percent. (Coghlan 1989)

Be Positive

Whether you are at home, in the workplace, or among friends, be the person who exudes optimism, and you will find it reflected right back at you.

IF YOU HAD a challenge ahead of you—whether you were trying to climb a mountain or just finish a project at work—what kind of people would you want to be surrounded with? Pessimistic people who reminded you why you were likely to fail, or optimistic people who gave you reasons you would succeed?

Think of the people you like to be around. Think of the people who are a joy to be around. What do they have in common? Are any of them pessimistic—continually expecting the worst to happen? No. We gravitate to people who approach life with pleasant expectations.

Living a satisfied life is one of the defining challenges of our life, and it is a challenge best met with optimism.

Scientists have a very hard time predicting a person's happiness based on the events he or she has experienced. Instead, a far better predictor of happiness than the number of good or bad events a person has endured are the beliefs and attitudes he or she maintains. (Chen 1996)

There Will Be an End, but You Can Be Prepared

One of the great sources of anxiety as we age is that we will never get a chance to do that thing we always wanted to do, or to finish that project we were working on years ago, or to mend the fences that may have fallen into disrepair as our relationships evolved. Don't wait until the end of your life to figure out what you wished you had done. Think of those things now and do them.

STUDENTS OFTEN WILL procrastinate. Assign them a paper, with two months to do it, and many will literally wait until the last day, cramming through their readings, making notes, and then charging through the writing. Not a moment of this process is enjoyed. It is a manic effort, with little concern for quality. Students who write their papers in a timely fashion, anticipate what needs to be done, and do the work in an orderly process never feel out of control, and can even enjoy themselves.

We live life like a student writing a paper—either as the procrastinator or the planner. The procrastinator feels out of control, and each passing year is a source of desperation. The planner finishes what needs to be done, and treats each passing year as a sign of accomplishment.

Research on senior citizens finds that those who are most comfortable with their own mortality do not ignore the matter, but prepare themselves for it. (Oates 1997)

63

How We See the World Is More Important Than How the World Is

What is the shape of the world, what condition is it in? Scientists, philosophers, and kings could offer a never-ending debate on the question. But there is no real grade for the world apart from the one you assign it.

SCIENTISTS DID a study in which they showed people a deck of playing cards. On each of these cards, however, something was wrong, something differed from the usual. The four of clubs was red, the five of diamonds had six diamonds. People were shown the cards and asked what they saw.

Were people surprised to see these obviously error-filled cards? They were not, because they didn't notice. When asked to describe the cards they were looking at, people answered they were looking at the five of diamonds or the four of clubs. They didn't mention that the cards were mismarked.

Why did this happen? Because what we see is a function not only of what is really there, but also of what we are looking for—our expectations, our assumptions.

People who have experienced similar life events can wind up with nearly opposite perceptions of life satisfaction. Researchers have compared, for example, people who have received a job promotion, and they found that while some of the people treasure the opportunity others lament the added responsibility. The implications of life events are a matter of perspective. (Chen 1996)

Keep a Pen and Paper Handy

People often feel frustrated that they can't remember a good idea they had last week or an interesting dream they had last night. Those who keep a notebook feel like they are more in control and are missing less.

EMILY IS an aspiring writer and is always writing things down. Even when she can't find paper, she scrambles to find envelopes, napkins, a piece of cardboard, anything that she can use to write down her thoughts. Does she do this because she is a particularly forgetful person? No, it is because she is both realistic enough and disciplined enough to know that human beings run across too many ideas in a day to remember all of them or even most of them. Good ideas come floating into our heads and will just as easily float right out. Writers who acknowledge this carry around a notebook so that the best of those ideas make it to paper. You don't have to be a writer, however, to have good ideas floating through you. Keep a notebook and pen handy, and you will be able to hold on to those fleeting thoughts.

While purposeful activity contributes to happiness, feelings of lost thoughts and opportunities contribute to an unhealthy frustration. People who feel like their best ideas escape them are 37 percent less likely to feel content than people who do not. (Madigan, Mise, and Maynard 1996)

Help the Next Person Who Needs Some Minor Assistance

G iving help is a win-win situation, so take the time to pay attention to your surroundings and offer the help that you can. It could be as simple as making a habit of holding the door open for the person coming in behind you. It's a gesture of friendliness that makes another person feel better and makes you feel good about yourself.

STACY MOVED to the Midwest from the Northeast and quickly noticed that people in the Midwest seemed to be in the habit of being courteous drivers. If you were stuck trying to get out of a parking lot, with a mile-long procession of cars in front of you on the main road, people in the Midwest would stop and give you room to pull out.

Based on their example, Stacy got in the habit of letting cars out when traffic was backed up. Stacy liked this friendly approach to life and soon received a dramatic example of its value.

After letting a car out in front of her, Stacy soon had to pull over to the side of the road because her car was making a strange noise. The driver she had let out saw her pull over and followed her. The other driver asked Stacy if she needed any help, and after a brief investigation concluded that Stacy had just run out of gas. He gave her enough gas to get her to a station and told her how nice he found people in this part of the country. She gave him her telephone number, and one year later they were married.

Life satisfaction was found to improve 24 percent with the level of altruistic activity. (Williams, Haber, Weaver, and Freeman 1998)

66

Take Care Not to Harshly Criticize Family and Friends

We rely on those closest to us for support. We can accept critical words from those who are not close to us because we can believe they reflect a lack of knowledge about us rather than an actual flaw in us. From our friends and family, however, critical words cut deeply. Try to avoid fixing your friends and family. Love them for who they are. If you must say something negative, always be constructive. Make your criticism reflect your love and respect, not your disappointment.

"WELL, THAT WAS stupid," Carol's mother said to her as Carol explained how she had lost a file at work and in the process made her boss angry at her. *Stupid.* The word flew out of her mother's mouth and slapped Carol in the head. She didn't like having her boss disappointed with her, but her own mother calling her stupid was painful.

Stupid is a common word, with a range of meanings from ill-considered to ignorant. Maybe Carol's mother meant it in the nicest possible terms, but even then, when speaking to someone, especially someone close, you have to assume that your words will be taken in the strongest, least positive way.

Aggression and fixations on disagreements reduces satisfaction in relationships by nearly 70 percent. (Chand 1990)

67

Some People Like the Big Picture, and Others Like the Details

When you look at a restaurant bill, you can eye the total due or you can focus on each item listed. Life is the same way. You can think in terms of the totality of what you have accomplished, or you can think in terms of the momentary episodes of your life. Adopt the focus that makes you feel more satisfied. If you think things turned out all right even though there were bumps in the road, think big picture. If you're not sure how it will turn out but you know that your life has been marked with moments of great happiness and pleasure, then focus on the details.

IT'S SATURDAY afternoon, and two men who live next door to each other in older homes of about the same size and condition are in their backyards. One is swinging in a hammock. The other is sweating in the sun, painting his fence. The man in the hammock is happy and comfortable knowing that his house will stand for many, many years, offering him and his family shelter. His neighbor is happy, too, because he is thinking about how sharp the fence will look with a little paint, and he takes satisfaction from how good the back door looks that he painted last week. One is taking comfort in the big picture, the other in the details. The important thing is that they find satisfaction.

Researchers find that it is not more typical to experience happiness as following from events or to experience our perspective on events as flowing from happiness; both patterns are prevalent. (Scherpenzeel and Saris 1996)

Do Things You Are Good At

W e need to feel competent. Take on responsibilities in areas in which you excel, whether it's cooking, gardening, or accounting, and ask for help when you are struggling.

RESEARCHERS AT PENN State noticed a rather pronounced trend in students' grades. In departments where students have fewer required courses, the students receive generally higher grades. At first the researchers assumed this was because those students took the easiest classes available. Then they found those students had higher grades in both their electives and their required classes.

The researchers concluded the root of this pattern was that by having more freedom to choose classes, students indeed tended to take courses they were interested in and that they could do well in. But, more important, doing well in those elective classes actually improved their performance in all their classes, because the positive habits that success created in the electives carried over into their required courses.

Who is happier, stay-at-home parents or parents who work outside the home? In studies comparing members of those two groups, researchers found happiness in both situations if the person felt competent at what they were doing. (Haw 1995)

Go Visit Your Neighbor

We no longer live in a time when people know all their neighbors and consider them to be friends. A shocking number of people have never had a conversation with their neighbors, and some couldn't pick them out of a lineup. Introduce yourself, or invite your neighbor over for coffee. Neighbors are not only a great potential source of friendship, they make us feel more comfortable in our homes, which is where most of us spend much of our time.

NEW HOUSES ARE being built across the country with an amazing new feature: front porches. According to the National Association of Home Builders, space that once might have been dedicated to a living room is now more likely to be used for a front porch.

Architects, builders, and town planners see the front porch as one remedy to the unhappy and uncomfortable social distance that characterizes many neighborhoods. Many of us don't know who our neighbors are, and often we don't know anything about them. This despite the fact that we have something tremendously important in common—our neighborhood, our surroundings, the place we begin and end each day. Front porches are making a comeback because most of us would like the chance to venture outside our front door and meet the people on our street.

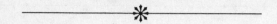

Greater community interactions can increase happiness by almost 30 percent. (Sugarman 1997)

Smile

Your smile makes other people happy, which in turn makes you happy.

IF YOU COULD do something that would make people happy, and it would cost you neither money nor time, would you do it? If that same thing also made you happy, would you do it? What is this magical thing that will brighten your day and the days of people around you and yet cost you nothing? A smile.

Scientists at the University of California in San Francisco have identified nineteen different kinds of smiles, each of them capable of communicating a pleasant message that will often be met with a smile in return.

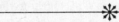

In a study of adults of various ages, a tendency was found for subjects to mimic the expressions of those around them. In other words, sad faces evoked more sad faces, and smiling faces evoked smiles and happiness. (Lundqvist and Dimberg 1995)

Don't Accept Television's Picture of the World

Watch television for any length of time, whether it's the news or a prime-time show, and you will inevitably come to the conclusion that virtually everyone is either very rich or about to die a horrible, bloody death. These pictures affect us more than we know. We fear that the awful events on television will happen to us, and we are frustrated that the nearly universal wealth we see on television hasn't reached us yet. Separate what you see from what you know to be real. Base your expectations on reality, not on television.

FOR A THOUSAND generations, the Gwinch'in tribe lived in northern Alaska in nearly complete isolation from outside cultures. Tribal members were completely self-sufficient, surviving on skills taught to them by their parents and elders.

In 1980, one of the tribe's leaders acquired a television.

Members of the tribe describe the event as the beginning of an addiction. Soon the native customs were ignored to maximize TV-watching time. One researcher said of the tribe's experience, "For these natives, like anyone else, television is a cultural nerve gas. It's odorless, painless and tasteless, and deadly."

What happened to the Gwinch'in traditions that had existed for thousands of years? In the words of one tribe member, "Television made us wish we were something else. It taught us greed and waste, and now everything that we were is gone."

Television changes our view of the world, and can encourage us to develop highly unrealistic and often damaging conclusions that serve to reduce our life satisfaction by up to 50 percent. (Jeffres and Dobos 1995)

72

You Always Have a Choice

Remember, you don't have to do anything. You can choose to do whatever you think is important enough to warrant your efforts. Don't lament your responsibilities as burdensome and unavoidable. Think of the positive effects of your actions—the reasons you go to work, the reasons you keep the household running.

HOW MANY TIMES have you complained to yourself, "Why do I have to do this?" Would you believe that you don't have to do it? Unless you are in prison, you don't have to do anything. You choose to do things.

You might ask, "What difference does that make? I have to do the laundry, or I choose to do the laundry. Either way it has to be done."

It makes a tremendous difference. It is the difference between taking an action because something of value is at stake for you, and taking an action because you are being forced to do so. Doing the laundry is a choice you make because you value being clean and presentable, or you do the laundry for your family members because you love them.

Every time we do the laundry we are doing it because we want to. Is anyone forcing you to do the laundry? No. When you see all the options you have, you can begin to appreciate the choices you make.

Interviews on life satisfaction levels found that those who expressed a sense of autonomy, of making decisions for themselves, were three times more likely to feel satisfied than those who did not. (Fisher 1995)

Be Agreeable

Make it easy for people to deal with you. Don't be angry or disruptive merely because you can.

SATURDAY MORNING, Frank went to play golf with his friend Mark. He told his wife, Michelle, that he'd be home around two. After golf, Mark asked Frank to help him move some furniture back at his place. After the furniture was moved, Mark offered Frank a sandwich, and soon the afternoon was slipping away. Frank looked at his watch as he drove home and was startled to see that it was after five. He hadn't called Michelle. He had said he'd be home hours ago, and he hadn't called. She was going to be mad. She probably had made some plans, and now he was hours late, and he hadn't called. This could easily turn into an argument, and then the whole night would be shot.

Frank walked through the door thinking of possible excuses, but instead he apologized and offered to make dinner. Michelle smiled, accepted his offer, and asked him how his day was. And they both happily enjoyed their evening.

Researchers found that having a positive attitude about those around us is among the most important predictors of life satisfaction and that without such attitudes, we are less than half as likely to feel happy. (Glass and Jolly 1997)

Don't Ignore One Part of Your Life

We are happier when all the pieces of our life are generally in good shape than when one area we care about is perfect and everything else is falling apart.

NOTICE THE WAY some organizations make decisions. They make them in separate units rather than thinking about the organization as a whole.

A university will assign a first-floor classroom for an early morning final exam despite the fact that the maintenance crew is at that very same time cutting the grass right outside the window. Why? The classroom was chosen by the dean because it was precisely the right size, while the maintenance workers were sent out by their manager because it's cooler in the mornings and therefore easier to work outside.

What's the result? The two tasks conflict with each other, and neither will be a success. The exam is disrupted by the noise, and ultimately the lawn cutting is stopped before it's finished to suit the needs of the students.

You have an advantage over an organization, though. You know about all your needs and priorities. Your task is to take all of them into account as you pursue your goals.

In research on a large group of college students, those who were less likely to link the attainment of a specific goal to their overall mood were 19 percent more likely to be satisfied. (Smith 1997)

Listen to Music

Music communicates to us on many different levels, and our favorite music tends to transport our mind to its favorite place.

DO YOU KNOW what happened when professors played Mozart to their classes while the students worked on a series of tests? The students did better. Why? Because scientists have found that music stimulates our brain.

Contrary to some reports that have suggested this effect occurs mainly with infants, the actual research suggests music has positive effects for any age. Music excites our mind, whether we are one, forty-one, or a hundred and one.

A positive effect on mood was found for 92 percent of individuals when they listened to the music of their choice. Excitement and happiness were typical reactions to the music. (Hakanen 1995)

Let Your Goals Guide You

When you have chosen reasonable, meaningful, and aligned goals, pursue them with all your heart.

IMAGINE YOURSELF in your kitchen, about to make something tremendous. Do you spend hours taking every product in your cabinet and every food in your refrigerator, pouring it all in one giant bowl, mixing it, baking it, and then putting it on your table? No doubt, even if you went to great effort at great expense, you would wind up with a giant inedible pile of garbage.

What if, instead, you carefully followed a recipe, went to the store to buy just what you needed, put in just the right amount of the perfect ingredients, and cooked it as instructed? Then you would wind up with exactly what you wanted.

Life works the same way. It doesn't take everything you have, and everything you can get your hands on, to wind up where you want to be. It takes a plan and the patience to follow the needed steps.

In ongoing interviews with a group of attorneys, a distinct transition was noted as career became less important and family more important. Those who recognized the change and reorganized their priorities accordingly expressed 29 percent more life satisfaction than those who did not. (Adams 1983)

Use Your Job Positively

At its best, work gives us a sense of purpose and enhances our appreciation of our life outside of the workplace. Appreciate all that your job gives you, and it will help you appreciate what really matters.

WISCONSIN HAS a new program that tries to place all the unemployed people in the state into jobs. Do you know what the people who get jobs like the most after they find themselves employed? It's not the money. It's the self-respect. They see their job as a chance to demonstrate their responsibility, their ability, their dependability, and they find that working makes all those things clear, not just to others but to themselves. Use your job, not as a sentence, not as punishment, but as a chance to show off—and show yourself—what you can do.

Research on over 1,500 mothers found that working outside the home increased life satisfaction 5 percent and contributed to a feeling of equality in the family. (Rogers 1996)

Don't Forget to Have Fun

Every day leave yourself some time to enjoy, to be silly, to laugh.

WATCH CHILDREN RUNNING around in the playground and you will soon be thinking, "They're having so much fun." Why are *they* having so much fun? The better question is, Why aren't *you* having more fun? Children run around and play as if by instinct. They do not question whether they should have fun, they just go out and do it. Adults have responsibilities. We're more serious. Ask one of your friends to do something fun with you, and you might hear, "I don't have time for that." Imagine a child being asked if she wanted to go to the zoo and answering, "I'll have to get back to you, I'm really swamped right now." Sometimes children know better than we do. Having a little fun, a time for pure silliness and happiness, is an essential part of every day.

Regularly having fun is one of the five central factors in leading a satisfied life. Individuals who spend time just having fun are 20 percent more likely to feel happy on a daily basis and 36 percent more likely to feel comfortable with their age and stage in life. (Lepper 1996)

Believe in Ultimate Justice

That there are many problems in the world is obvious to anyone, but take comfort in the notion that eventually good prevails. Whether your focus is on the criminal justice system or a spiritual system, realize that those who have wronged the world will eventually pay some price.

JOHN LIST WAS a mild-mannered, unremarkable-looking older man. The kind you saw on the street and didn't give a second thought to. One day a television show did a story on John List. Decades earlier, this unremarkable man had committed a heinous crime, murdering his family. He assumed another life and hid from his crime for decades.

Did he "get away with it" all those years? Well, he certainly wasn't in prison, but he later described the personal hell of waiting every moment for the mask to be broken and for his new world to crumble.

Regardless of the experiences subjects personally dealt with, whether they had personally been the victim of a crime or known someone close who had, those who believed the world is ultimately just retained a 13 percent higher level of life satisfaction. (Lipkus, Dalbert, and Siegler 1996)

Reminisce

Think of the happy times you, your family, and friends have had together. Recalling happiness of the past has the powerful ability to bring us happiness in the present.

NEIL CAME OVER on a boat when he was fourteen years old. He came by himself to a new country where he didn't know anyone. He got a job as a handyman, working for the mayor of a small East Coast city. It was an old-time political machine, and the mayor seemed to run everything in town. Neil would tell his grandchildren story after story about his trip to America and his early years working for the mayor.

This was his favorite story: Neil was walking across town in a frayed suit from the thrift shop that was two sizes too small. The mayor saw Neil walking by and asked him where he was going. Neil said he was on his way to the church; that he was about to be married. The mayor looked him up and down and said he should have a proper suit to be married in. Neil was embarrassed and told the mayor he did not have enough money to buy new clothes. The mayor told Neil that today he would be the best-dressed man in the city, and he quickly whisked him off to the tailor. The tailor's shop was closed. The mayor sent the police to find the tailor, who came in because the mayor asked him. The tailor made a fine set of clothes for Neil and asked Neil for no money.

Neil never grew tired of recounting his pride and excitement from that day—that the mayor had showed him such kindness and that he had not been a disappointment to his bride. No matter how many times Neil told the story, it brought him a warm feeling inside.

When people consciously choose to think back on their past, over 80 percent tend to focus on very positive memories. (Hogstel and Curry 1995)

Be Conscientious

Finish what you start. Care about what you are doing, and do it right. Although being conscientious is not as easy as slacking off, we feel better about ourselves when we do a good job.

LOCALS LOVE to tell the story of the bridge to nowhere. In southwest Florida, engineers had designed one of the biggest bridges in the state. The bridge was so big that they had to build it by starting on both banks and building toward the center. Trouble is, when they reached the middle, the two sides didn't meet. They were two feet apart. Millions upon millions of dollars, and thousands upon thousands of worker-hours, and the whole thing didn't work. You know what they did? They built a second new bridge.

It's an old saying, but it still applies. There are two ways to do something: take some time and do it right, or hurry the job and never finish.

Research on adults reveals that a tendency to be disciplined, deliberate, and dutiful has an 18 percent positive effect on happiness. (Furnham and Cheng 1997)

Don't Dwell on Unwinnable Conflicts

M ove on. The problems you spend your time and energy on should be both important and improvable. Otherwise, you are better off moving on to things you can change.

IN MYTHOLOGY, Sisyphus was doomed to the endless task of pushing a boulder up a hill. Just before he got it to the top he would lose his hold, and the boulder would roll back down to the bottom. Sisyphus would push the boulder up again and almost have it to the top before it fell back. There was, of course, no point. It was just a death sentence.

Some of us approach our disagreements and disappointments as if they were Sisyphus's boulder. We push and push and push and never consider that there is no point. The beauty of real life, though, is that our boulders are of our own creation and will disappear if we just stop pushing.

Many people experience conflict in balancing their time between work and home. Studies find that people who want to spend more time in both settings wind up feeling decreased satisfaction at home and at work. Those who recognize that their limited time is a conflict without a readily available solution are one-fourth more likely to feel comfortable with themselves than those who do not. (Caproni 1997)

Enjoy the Ordinary

You do countless things in the average day that can be labeled as chores or can be relabeled as enjoyable. Walking the dog is something that has to be done, yes, but while you walk the dog you get some pleasant exercise, some time to think, and a chance to see the neighbors and the neighborhood. Enjoy what you do every day.

WE KNOW most days will be regular days. Our lives will include some highlight days that stay with us forever, like family celebrations or personal triumphs, but almost every day this year will be a regular day, with nothing particularly astounding about it.

Yet within these regular days are many opportunities for enjoyment, many of which we don't even think about or really appreciate. Take a moment every day to think about the simple pleasures of your daily life.

Take Lonnie, for example, who recently enjoyed his 103rd birthday. Lonnie sat in a rocking chair on his front porch, gently rocking back and forth as reporters asked him how he felt on this special day. He said he felt great because every day was special to him.

In a study of over thirteen thousand people, 96 percent of subjects rated their satisfaction with life typically no higher than "fairly positive." The satisfied life was not one of extremes but of steady, generally positive feelings. (Diener and Diener 1995)

84

Focus Not on the World's Tragedies, but on the World's Hope

M any sad things happen in our world, but rather than focusing on them, have hope for the future. Think of the world's potential. Perhaps the future holds the curing of diseases, the end of violence, the amelioration of poverty and hunger.

THE SAN JACINTO Girl Scout Council wanted to do something fun, exciting, and uniting in their community. They decided to try to create the world's largest friendship circle, a circle of people holding hands in a celebration of community.

The Girl Scouts invited local residents to join them, and on a Saturday morning at a nearby amusement park, they set up their circle. The mayor of Houston as well as 6,243 other people participated in the event. The circle stretched out for over a mile, as people joined hands to celebrate the group's message that "friendship conquers hatred." One Girl Scout leader said the day's events were meant to "teach girls and adults that everybody matters, and to value differences among ourselves."

As a nine-year-old scout explained, "It's important to be a friend to everybody because you could hurt somebody's feelings."

Over nine in ten Americans are uncomfortable or worried about aspects of the world and of society. The difference between more and less happy people is what they do with that discomfort. Less happy people wallow in the problems they see, while happier people focus on potential improvements in the future. (Garrett 1996)

Get a Hobby

Hobbies are a steady source of interest, providing two essential ingredients in life: consistency and fun.

ELSA COLLECTS old books. She has all sorts of books lining the shelves of her home, some classics, some rare first editions, and some she just likes to page through. For Elsa, collecting books is a source of entertainment and a source of connection to all sorts of people she meets. Every town she visits is a potential source of adventure as she visits antique shops and used bookstores, looking to add to her collection. What does collecting books mean to Elsa? "It puts me in touch with history, it puts me in touch with other people who I meet and trade books with, and most important, I just like having books around."

In surveys of thousands of adults, those who had a hobby were found to be 6 percent more likely to rate their lives favorably. (Mookherjee 1997)

Envying Other People's Relationships Is Pointless

People with many friends sometimes yearn for a closer family, and people with a close family sometimes yearn for more friends. The key to continued satisfaction with life is not in replicating what someone else has. Instead, build a support system that you draw from and give to, regardless of whether it is made up primarily of friends or family.

A GROUP of philosophers and historians gathered a few years back to study the advantages of family life two centuries ago. They were concerned about the instability in our current family situations and the widespread fear that our society is suffering from the lack of traditional family relationships. The academics wondered if the agrarian family unit—a stable mother-father bond and a large group of siblings—was really ideal for humans and if any of the lessons from yesteryear could be applied today.

Here's what they concluded: today we envy the traditional family for its cohesion and stability, while two hundred years ago members of the traditional family often felt that their individuality was overwhelmed by their family unit—that they were not really a full person, just a cog in the family machine.

The irony of this situation was not lost on the researchers. Today many of us yearn for more contact with our family, while two hundred years ago people had so much contact with their families that they became sick of one another. The best hope is to enjoy the relationships you have, neither forcing them to meet some artificial standard nor holding them up for comparison with anyone else's life and loves.

In research on over 8,000 adults, researchers considered over 100 factors that contribute to happiness. Among the factors that had a major negative effect was the use of comparisons that implied personal failures in relationships, which reduced happiness by 26 percent. (Li, Young, Wei, Zhang, Zheng, Xiao, Wang, and Chen 1998)

Give Yourself Time to Adapt to Change

Don't expect to be immediately comfortable after a move or in a new situation. Give yourself time to adjust. If you learn how to ease yourself into new circumstances, changes you make in the future will be easier for you.

JILL IS A RESPECTED veteran teacher, having taught eighth-graders for over twenty years. Teachers have a unique job in that each year they begin again and are surrounded by an entirely new cast of characters. Even though Jill was experienced and loved teaching, every year she had the same ritual the night before the first day of school. She tossed and turned, worried and wondered, and barely slept at all.

Jill acknowledges the human instinct to be uncomfortable with change and lets herself be nervous about meeting twenty-five new faces that first day. Soon, though, she takes comfort in the familiar aspects that remain constant, and she recharges with the notion that she is about to embark on a new adventure, unlike any she has taken before.

In a study of newly married couples, those couples who acknowledged the difficulties of their new situation were 1.5 times more comfortable with each other, and with marriage, than those who tried to conceal the difficulty of dealing with change. (Monteiro 1991)

Focus on What Really Matters to You

There is no point in competing in a game that you do not really care to win. Don't allow your life and expectations to become anything but deeply personal reflections of what matters the most to you.

THE 1999 WINNER of the Nathan's Hot Dog Eating Contest was accused of cheating. They say he started to eat his first hot dog before the twelve-minute time limit began. When time was up, he had consumed twenty and one-quarter hot dogs, while the second place finisher had eaten twenty. The matter is of great importance to the top two finishers. Each desperately wants to be the hot dog eating champion.

Would you enter a hot dog eating contest, which requires you to prepare by regularly eating unhealthy amounts of food in a short period of time? Probably not, because your hot dog eating abilities are not something you really pride yourself on, not something that really matters to you.

Yet many of us are constantly in competitions where we don't really want the prize. We find someone to be in a secret economic competition with—a friend, a neighbor, a loved one.

We size up their home, their car, their lifestyle and try to do them one better. But our life is not changed for the better if the engine falls out of their car or if they suddenly have to cancel a vacation because of finances. Others look around at work for a rival and measure their relative progress against the other person.

But is this really your goal? Were you born into this world to get pro-moted before one of your co-workers? Were you born into this world to get a better car than your neighbors? Let your real goals guide you, not meaningless competitions you don't really benefit by winning.

Goals are crucial to one's orientation to the world and to life satisfaction. If one's goals conform to one's self-concept, it increases by 43 percent the likelihood that goals will contribute in a positive fashion to life satisfaction. (Emmons and Kaiser 1996)

89

Realize That Complete Satisfaction Does Not Exist

Set your sights on being generally satisfied and generally happy, not on expecting every aspect of life to be perfect. Complete satisfaction does not exist because everything can be improved upon. Those who accept this can appreciate what they have. Those who do not accept this can never appreciate what they have even as their circumstances improve. Strive to improve. Don't try to be perfect.

"GOLF," ACCORDING to Mark Twain, "is a good walk spoiled." Golf is perhaps the most frustrating of all games. It seems so simple. A white ball— stationary, for goodness' sake! You swing a club, the ball flies, you walk to the ball, and you do it again. The problem with hitting a golf ball is that because it requires an almost infinite series of body contortions, club movements, and angles, it always results in a less than perfect shot.

If you listen to people who play golf for fun, you will hear them say, "Just let me get one birdie. Just one birdie, and I will be happy." A birdie is the score you get when you hit the ball in the hole in one less shot than it would take the average professional to do it. And do you know what happens when they get that first birdie? They say, "Just one more birdie." Every improvement in their game is inexorably followed by the demand for further improvement.

Golf equipment makers know that players are so desperate they will try to buy their way to improvement. As one manufacturer explained, "You'll never run out of things to sell a golfer. Golfers would buy a swing if they could, especially if it would let them hit the ball straight and toward the target every time."

But they can never, ever reach perfection. That's right, even professional golfers spend their entire careers hitting less than perfect shots.

Those who believe they will fail to achieve their goals are unhappy, but so too are those who believe they will exactly meet their goals. Those who are happiest believe they will meet some of their goals and will receive satisfaction from multiple aspects of their lives. (Chen 1996)

90

Surround Yourself with Pleasant Aromas

Here's a simple way to make yourself feel better. Air out your house and add some fragrant flowers. Make your home smell nice, and you will feel the effects.

FIVE HUNDRED YEARS ago, soldiers in Europe used good-smelling spices to distract the injured from their pain. Today, doctors are experimenting with aromatherapy in the hospital, using good smells to comfort those in postoperative recovery.

Bad smells are crafty characters. They get in our lives, and they never leave. If you live with them long enough, you can't even notice them, because they've been around too long. An old musty carpet or some other source of odor is really an attack on our senses. Not noticing the smell is not the same as the smell not being there. We've just surrendered our sense of smell and our brain, unwilling to continue processing something so unpleasant.

Good smells, on the other hand, as soldiers knew in the fifteenth century, and doctors are rediscovering today, awaken the senses and the brain and at a subconscious level remind us of good things.

Our senses operate all the time, offering us important signals about our environment. Pleasant smells evoke surprise and happiness for more than eight out of ten individuals, while unpleasant odors trigger disgust and unhappy reactions. (Alaoui-Ismaieli, Robin, Rada, Dittmar, and Vernet-Maury 1997)

91

Don't Let Others Set Your Goals

Too many people choose goals based on what others think. Instead, think about what you really care about, and set meaningful goals to accomplish what matters to you.

GARY LEFT the military after twenty years of service as a marine pilot. His military friends were surprised that he would leave with the possibility of promotion dangling in front of him. How could he do this? What was wrong with him? His friends didn't quite say this to him, but that is what they wanted to know.

Gary had an answer. "Holding the highest rank has never been my dream," he said. "It might be your dream, and that's fine, but it isn't mine."

Gary's dream was to serve his country by serving children. He offered his services to the local school district, and in a matter of a few years was asked to run a new and rigorous high school academic program. Learning, according to Gary, is a lot like flying. "You have your hands on the controls, you have the power to excel. It's all within your hands." Teaching is, for him, a dream come true, a dream that could never have come true if Gary had worried about what other people thought he should do.

People do not have to succeed in absolutely everything they do to feel happy. But, people do have to believe they have maintained control over their own life. In fact, those who feel that they were responsible for their own position and decisions express one-third more life satisfaction than those who do not. (Kean, Van Zandt, and Miller 1996)

92

You Are a Person, Not a Stereotype

People are happiest when they allow their individual personality to come out, not when they conform to popular images. Men who believe they must act tough and women who believe they must act soft are boxed in to a set of expectations that have nothing to do with who they are.

LOOK AROUND at a funeral, and you will see women crying and men standing with steely faces. Men have been taught to be tough, not to reveal their emotions. Women have been taught to be more open, more expressive. The National Institutes of Health has documented that with both physical and emotional pain, men are much less likely than women to reveal their discomfort.

It is important to remember, though, that not all of us fit those expectations.

A man who wants to cry at a funeral but stops himself because he's been taught to be tough is not really being tough. He's pretending to be what he thinks people expect of him. A woman who forces herself to open up in front of others but who would rather act more reserved is not a nicer person for showing her emotions and will not be happier for having to act in a way that is unnatural to her.

You have to act the way you think is appropriate, not the way you think the average man or woman is supposed to act. Our generalizations about men and women are often false and too often damaging.

Satisfaction with life was not found to be connected to how well men and women fit into gender stereotypes of femininity and masculinity. (Ramanaiah, Detwiler, and Byravan 1995)

93

Know What Makes You Happy and Sad

People feel worse if they are unhappy but have no idea why. Think about your feelings and emotions. Then, even when you are unhappy, you will take comfort in knowing the cause and how it can be changed.

PROFESSOR JOHN HAMLER teaches a course on scientific thinking. He demystifies science on the first day of the class with the first words he says: "All science is noticing patterns."

He explains to his students that scientists see the world in a very orderly way. They look for what goes with what. Events and conditions are not random; they have causes and effect. "Science is noticing patterns, great and small. What happens when you throw a rock up in the air? It comes back down every time. That is a pattern; that is the essence of science."

The difference between most people and scientists, Professor Hamler explains, "is that people let the world be random to them. They allow events to pass without connecting them to other events. Whatever happens, it just happens, there's nothing else to it. Scientists everywhere, all the time, see connections because they are looking for connections."

In dealing with our own emotions and life satisfaction, we need to be scientists. We need to notice patterns. Those who let themselves exist in the midst of random events not only don't understand what is happening to them, they also can't do anything to change their world.

Those who are least likely to quickly overcome a temporary sense of dissatisfaction with life are those who cannot define the sources of their feelings. (Ramanaiah and Detwiler 1997)

94

Keep Reading

Those who read books benefit from what they learn and the entertainment they receive. But in addition, they get to exercise their brain, and when we do that, we feel satisfied that we are spending our time wisely.

WHICH WOULD YOU choose to be, a person with an ever-decreasing attention span, or a person with an ever-increasing attention span? A person with access to the second- and third-rate work that would have been considered trash two decades ago, or a person with access to the work of the greatest minds we have ever known? A person with access to a perpetual run of the same basic story with the same basic characters, or a person with access to an array of choices that span nearly an infinite imagination? A person who likely won't be able to remember a story ten minutes later, or a person who might carry a tale for the rest of his or her life?

Which would you rather be, a person who usually spends his or her free time in front of the television, or a person who usually spends his or her free time reading?

Reading engages the mind. Reading materials, by exercising our memory and imagination, can contribute to happiness in ways similar to active positive thinking. Regular readers are about 8 percent more likely to express daily satisfaction. (Scope 1999)

We Must Feel Needed

Think of those who rely on your friendship, caring, guidance, help. You probably don't realize how important you are to the people in your life.

THE LABOR DEPARTMENT has done a study on older workers to find out what keeps them coming to work and what encourages them to retire. One of the most often cited reasons for stopping work is not that they are tired or want to spend more time in their garden. What often sends older folks into retirement is the feeling that they are no longer needed on the job. Workers retired when they felt that their purpose was in doubt, that others could do what they could do better, and that they were only taking up space. They left because they were no longer needed.

Think about what this means for our personal lives. Even though we can't retire from our personal lives, we still need to feel needed. Remember how much other people matter to you, and realize that you matter to them just as much.

In an experimental research program, a relationship was found between happiness and helping behavior. By helping others, we create positive bonds with people and enhance our self-image. Those who had more opportunities to offer help felt 11 percent better about themselves. (Pegalis 1994)

Say "So What?"

A classmate at your high school reunion is richer, prettier, smarter, than everybody else. Does it matter? No. Your life is shaped more by your everyday relationships than by the lives of acquaintances you see only rarely.

TWO FRIENDS from high school, Ken and Alan, went off to college and on to separate careers. Alan became a social worker, helping distressed families. Ken became a computer consultant, founded his own company, and became super-rich.

Alan loved his job and felt great about the impact he was able to make on the families he worked with. But with Ken in the news—newspapers covering his company's success and his growing fortune—Alan began to question his choices.

How could someone he know be so rich while he lived such a modest life? Why didn't he have Ken's success?

The truth is, Alan didn't *want* Ken's success. He was never interested in dedicating his life to a corporation, and he didn't spend his days dreaming of riches. He wanted to help people, and he was helping people. His jealousy of Ken's life faded away as he looked at the smiling faces of the children he helped every day.

Sometimes we look at what other people have and we want that instead of thinking about what really and truly motivates us, what we really and truly want and need. Don't take someone else's accomplishment as evidence that you are doing anything wrong.

Satisfaction with life was found to be related to experiences with family and friends—those with regular participation in one's life—and to be unrelated to those with whom contact is brief or irregular. (Hong and Duff 1997)

97

Have a Purpose

Without a purpose nothing matters. You can work forty hours a week, come home to cook, clean, and then take up seventy-two new good habits, but if there isn't a reason you are doing it, none of these activities will mean anything to you.

SAY YOU'RE a student. Why should you study for a test? To do well in the course. Why do you care if you do well in the course? So you can get a degree. Why do you care if you get a degree? Because it will help you get a good job. Now, the job may be years away, but it is the foundation upon which all your efforts are based. Take away the eventual outcome, and all the steps in between become just killing time. Why bother doing any of these things if they are not leading toward something you care about? It's more fun to goof off than study for the test, and if there is nothing at stake, then we goof off.

It is much easier to apply yourself to the activities you do for your family or your personal success if you define what you want and are able to see how what you are doing is leading you forward.

In research on college students, a comparison was made between students who enjoyed their lives and studies and students who were least comfortable with their environment. A major difference between the two groups was a sense of underlying purpose in life, which almost twice as many of the former group had. (Rahman and Khaleque 1996)

98

You Have Not Finished the Best Part of Your Life

We hear that youth is wasted on the young. People who say this are accepting the myth that only the young can enjoy life to the fullest. The truth is that older people do not consider their young days to be their best days; most enjoy their senior years more than any other part of their life.

WARREN WAS a middle-aged professor. Comfortable in all respects, he anticipated that he would continue teaching for many years. The college faced a budget shortfall, however, and took the unprecedented step of eliminating a number of its academic departments, including Warren's.

For Warren, everything seemed to have been destroyed. Everything he counted on was gone, and he felt too old to start all over again. Too old to search for another college to employ him, and too old to restart his life.

Instead of giving up, Warren realized how much the world had to offer. Instead of concluding that he had suffered a loss that could never be replaced, he chose to focus on the opportunity set before him. Never before had he had the chance to start again, to decide what he wanted to do and where he wanted to do it.

He wound up taking a year off from the world to live in a rural town. And how did he feel at the end of the year? "I've never been better."

Researchers conducted a long-term study of northern Californians, interviewing subjects multiple times over three decades. When asked when they had been the happiest in their lives, each time eight out of ten answered "right now." (Field 1997)

99

Money Does Not Buy Happiness

Whe spend so much time chasing dollars, worrying about dollars, and counting dollars. It may surprise you to learn that satisfaction with life is no more likely among the rich.

CONSIDER THIS for a moment: in this country, more people buy lottery tickets than vote. We all want to be rich. At least we all think we want to be rich. But lottery winners often find that instead of enjoying a lifetime of happiness because of their wealth, they face family feuds and disputes with friends. These events take away much of what the winner really valued in the first place. Ask one Illinois man who won $13 million, then weeks later received divorce papers and a demand for half the money from his wife.

There is a new movement in the United States called the minimalists. These are people who have decided to live on less money. They buy less, spend less, make less, and have less stuff. They also spend less time at work and more time with their friends and family. The minimalists have made a conscious conclusion that money did not buy them what they wanted most. They don't chase after money just because most people do.

Remember, if money could buy happiness, there would be high-priced happiness stores on every block.

A study of life satisfaction looked at twenty different factors that might contribute to happiness. Nineteen of those factors did matter, and one did not. The one factor that did not matter was financial status. (Hong and Giannakopoulos 1995)

100

What Does It All Mean? You Decide

Your future—how you feel about it, yourself, and everything else—follows from the decisions you make, the priorities you develop, and the perspective you see things through.

GREAT UNANSWERED QUESTIONS plague us, century after century. Why are we here? What are we supposed to be doing? What does this all matter? Answers to these questions are so very hard to come by because the truth lies not within someone else, but within you. You have been given life, and with it you have been given the opportunity to define it. Your life's path and purpose will be drawn on a map created by you.

In a study that followed the exploits of over 100 adults for a period of two years, it was found that the effect of "good" and "bad" events quickly faded. That is, subjects' happiness was not dependent on the sum of events but on what they made of those events. (Suh, Diener, and Fujita 1996)

Sources

Abdel Khalek, A., O. Al-Meshaan, and A. Al-Shatti. 1995. "Themes of Presleep Thoughts." *Journal of the Social Sciences* 23:63.

Acquino, J., D. Russell, C. Cutrona, and E. Altmaier. 1996. "Employment Status, Social Support, and Life Satisfaction." *Journal of Counseling Psychology* 43:480.

Adams, D. 1983. "The Psychological Development of Professional Black Women's Lives and the Consequences of Career for Their Personal Happiness." Ph.D. dissertation, Wright Institute, Berkeley, California.

Aine, D., and D. Lester. 1995. "Exercise, Depression, and Self-Esteem." *Perceptual and Motor Skills* 81:890.

Al-Amri, A., and M. Lee. 1996. "The Relationship Between Job Satisfaction and Life Satisfaction." *Journal of the Social Sciences* 24:289.

Alaoui-Ismaieli, O., O. Robin, H. Rada, A. Dittmar, and E. Vernet-Maury. 1997. "Basic Emotions Evoked by Odorants." *Physiology and Behavior* 62:713.

Argyle, M., M. Martin, and L. Lu. 1995. "Testing for Stress and Happiness: The Role of Social and Cognitive Factors." In *Stress and Emotion.* Washington, DC: Taylor and Francis.

Bailey, R., and C. Miller. 1998. "Life Satisfaction and Life Demands in College Students." *Social Behavior and Personality* 26:51.

Barofsky, I., and A. Rowan. 1998. "Models for Measuring Quality of Life: Implications for Human-Animal Interaction Research." In *Companion Animals in Human Health.* Thousand Oaks, CA: Sage.

Bartels, K. 1991. "Humor, Fitness, Happiness, and Cardiorespiratory After Pulse as Components of Wellness." Ph.D. dissertation, Iowa State University, Ames.

Battmann, W. 1996. "Resources, Stability and the Pursuit of Happiness." In *Processes of the Molar Regulation of Behavior.* Scottsdale, AZ: Pabst Science.

Bhargava, S. 1995. "An Integration-Theoretical Analysis of Life Satisfaction." *Psychological Studies* 40:170.

Bless, H., G. Clore, N. Schwarz, and V. Golisano. 1996. "Mood and the Use of Scripts." *Journal of Personality and Social Psychology* 71:665.

Botwin, M., D. Buss, and T. Shackelford. 1997. "Personality and Mate Preferences." *Journal of Personality* 65:107.

Brebner, J. 1995. "Testing for Stress and Happiness: The Role of Personality Factors." In *Stress and Emotion: Anxiety, Anger, and Curiosity.* Washington, DC: Taylor and Francis.

Brebner, J., J. Donaldson, N. Kirby, and L. Ward. 1995. "Relationships Between Happiness and Personality." *Personality and Individual Differences* 19:251.

Brebner, J., E. Greenglass, P. Laungani, and A. O'Roark. 1996. *Stress and Emotion: Anxiety, Anger, and Curiosity.* Washington, DC: Taylor and Francis.

Brown, J., and K. Dutton. 1995. "The Thrill of Victory, the Complexity of Defeat: Self-Esteem and People's Emotional Reaction to Success and Failure." *Journal of Personality and Social Psychology* 68:712.

Caproni, P. 1997. "Work/Life Balance: You Can't Get There from Here." *Journal of Applied Behavioral Science* 33:46.

Cautela, J., and W. Ishaq. 1996. *Contemporary Issues in Behavior Therapy: Improving the Human Condition.* New York: Plenum.

Chand, M. 1990. "An Inquiry into the Factors of a Successful Marriage." Ph.D. dissertation, Jadavpur University, Calcutta, India.

Chang, E., and A. Maydeu-Olivares. 1997. "Optimism and Pessimism as Partially Independent Constructs: Relationship to Positive and Negative Affectivity and Psychological Well-Being." *Personality and Individual Differences* 23:433.

Chebat, J., C. Gelinas-Chebat, A. Vaninski, and P. Filiatrault. 1995. "The Impact of Mood on Time Perception, Memorization, and Acceptance of Waiting." *Genetic, Social, and General Psychology* 121:411.

Chen, N. 1996. "Individual Differences in Answering the Four Questions for Happiness." Ph.D. dissertation, University of Georgia, Athens.

172

Chumbler, N. 1996. "An Empirical Test of a Theory of Factors Affecting Life Satisfaction." *Journal of Psychology and Theology* 24:220.

Clark, F., M. Carlson, R. Zemke, F. Gelya, K. Patterson, and B. L. Ennevor. 1996. "Life Domains and Adaptive Strategies of a Group of Low Income, Well Older Adults." *American Journal of Occupational Therapy* 50:99.

Clark, A., A. Oswald, and P. Warr. 1996. "Is Job Satisfaction U-Shaped in Age?" *Journal of Occupational and Organizational Psychology* 69:57.

Coghlan, C. 1989. "An Examination of Community Action Participation." Master's thesis, University of Texas, Arlington.

Condon, R. 1997. "Happiness and Worthwhileness." Ph.D. dissertation, University of California, Los Angeles.

Cramer, D. 1995. "Life and Job Satisfaction." *Journal of Psychology* 129:261.

Crist-Houran, M. 1996. "Efficacy of Volunteerism." *Psychological Reports* 79:736.

Daley, A., and G. Parfitt. 1996. "Good Health—Is It Worth It? Mood States, Physical Well-Being, Job Satisfaction and Absenteeism in Members and Non-members of a Health and Fitness Club." *Journal of Occupational and Organizational Psychology* 69:121.

Diener, E., and C. Diener. 1996. "Most People Are Happy." *Psychological Science* 7:181.

Diener, E., and M. Diener. 1995. "Cross-Cultural Correlates of Life Satisfaction and Self-Esteem." *Journal of Personality and Social Psychology* 68:653.

Diener, E., and F. Fujita. 1995. "Resources, Personal Strivings, and Subjective Well-Being." *Journal of Personality and Social Psychology* 68:926.

Emmons, R., and H. Kaiser. 1996. "Goal Orientation and Emotional Well-Being: Linking Goals and Affect Through the Self." In *Striving and Feeling.* Mahwah, NJ: Erlbaum.

Falkenberg, A. 1998. "Quality of Life." *Journal of Socio-Economics* 27:1.

Fernandez-Dols, J., and M. Ruiz-Belda. 1995. "Are Smiles a Sign of Happiness?" *Journal of Personality and Social Psychology* 69:1113.

Ferroni, P., and J. Taffe. 1997. "Women's Emotional Well-Being." *Sexual and Marital Therapy* 12:127.

Field, D. 1997. "Looking Back, What Period of Your Life Brought You the Most Satisfaction?" *International Journal of Aging and Human Development* 45:169.

Finch, J., M. Barrera, M. Okun, W. Bryant, G. Pool, and A. Snow-Turek. 1997. "The Factor Structure of Received Social Support: Dimensionality and the Prediction of Depression and Life Satisfaction." *Journal of Social and Clinical Psychology* 16:323.

Fisher, B. 1995. "Successful Aging, Life Satisfaction, and Generativity in Later Life." *International Journal of Aging and Human Development* 41:239.

Fontane, P. 1996. "Exercise, Fitness, and Feeling Well." *American Behavior Scientist* 39:288.

Forest, K. 1996. "Gender and Pathways to Subjective Well-Being." *Social Behavior and Personality* 24:19.

Francis, L., L. Brown, and D. Lester. 1998. "Happiness as Stable Extraversion." *Personality and Individual Differences* 24:167.

Furnham, A., and H. Cheng. 1997. "Personality and Happiness." *Psychological Reports* 80:761.

Garrett, R. 1996. "Wisdom as the Key to a Better World." In *Contemporary Issues in Behavior Therapy.* New York: Plenum.

Gerwood, J., M. LeBlanc, and N. Piazza. 1998. "The Purpose in Life Test and Religious Denomination." *Journal of Clinical Psychology* 54:49.

Gilovich, T., and V. Medvec. 1995. "Some Counterfactual Determinants of Satisfaction and Regret." *In What Might Have Been.* Mahwah, NJ: Erlbaum.

Glass, J. C., and G. Jolly. 1997. "Satisfaction in Later Life." *Educational Gerontology* 23:297.

Grove, K. 1987. "The Paradox of Happiness." Ph.D. dissertation, University of California, San Diego.

Hagedorn, J. 1996. "Happiness and Self-Deception: An Old Question Examined by a New Measure of Subjective Well-Being." *Social Indicators Research* 38:139.

Hakanen, E. 1995. "Emotional Use of Music by African American Adolescents." *Howard Journal of Communications* 5:124.

Haw, C. 1995. "The Family Life Cycle." *Psychological Medicine* 25:727.

Heatey, K., and D. Thombs. 1997. "Fruit-Vegetable Consumption Self-Efficacy in Youth." *American Journal of Health Behavior* 21:172.

Henry, C., and S. Lovelace. 1995. "Family Resources and Adolescent Family Life Satisfaction in Remarried Family Households." *Journal of Family Issues* 16:765.

Hogstel, M., and L. Curry. 1995. "Ego Integrity Versus Despair in Later Years." *Journal of Clinical Geropsychology* 1:165.

Hong, L., and R. Duff. 1997. "Relative Importance of Spouses, Children and Friends in the Life Satisfaction of Retirement Community Residents." *Journal of Clinical Geropsychology* 3:275.

Hong, S., and E. Giannakopoulos. 1995. "Students' Perceptions of Life Satisfaction." *College Student Journal* 29:438.

Hsieh, C. 1997. "Financial Well-Being and Happiness Among Middle Age and Old Age Americans." Ph.D. dissertation, University of Pennsylvania, Philadelphia.

Hunter, M., and K. L. Liao. 1995. "Problem-Solving Groups for Mid-Aged Women in General Practice." *Journal of Reproductive and Infant Psychology* 13:147.

Jacob, M., and V. Guarnaccia. 1997. "Motivational and Behavioral Correlates of Life Satisfaction." *Psychological Reports* 80:811.

Jeffres, L., and J. Dobos. 1995. "Separating People's Satisfaction with Life and Public Perceptions of the Quality of Life in the Environment." *Social Indicators Research* 34:181.

Jou, Y., and H. Fukada. 1997. "Stress and Social Support in Mental and Physical Health." *Psychological Reports* 81:1303.

Judge, T., E. Locke, C. Durham, and A. Kluger. 1998. "Dispositional Effects on Job and Life Satisfaction." *Journal of Applied Psychology* 83:17.

Kean, R., S. Van Zandt, and N. Miller. 1996. "Exploring Factors of Perceived Social Performance, Health and Personal Control."*International Journal of Aging and Human Development* 43:297.

Kehn, D. 1995. "Predictors of Elderly Happiness." *Activities, Adaptation, and Aging* 19:11.

Krug-Fite, J. 1992. "Predicting Marital Happiness from Personality Differences Between Partners." Ph.D. dissertation, Georgia State University, Atlanta.

Kwan, V., and M. Bond. 1997. "Pancultural Explanations for Life Satisfaction." *Journal of Personality and Social Psychology* 73:1038.

Lackovic-Grgin, K., and M. Dekovic. 1996. "Social Support and Self-Esteem in Unemployed University Graduates." *Adolescence* 31:701.

Lanier, L., G. Privette, S. Vodanovich, and C. Bundrick. 1996. "Peak Experiences." *Journal of Social Behavior and Personality* 11:781.

Lepper, H. 1996. "In Pursuit of Happiness and Satisfaction in Later Life: A Study of Competing Theories of Subjective Well-Being." Ph.D. dissertation, University of California, Riverside.

Li, L., D. Young, H. Wei, Y. Zhang, Y. Zheng, S. Xiao, Wang, and X. Chen. 1998. "The Relationship Between Objective Life Status and Subjective Life Satisfaction with Quality of Life." *Behavioral Medicine* 23:149.

Lindeman, M., and M. Verkasalo. 1996. "Meaning in Life." *Journal of Social Psychology* 136:657.

Lipkus, I., C. Dalbert, and I. Siegler. 1996. "The Importance of Distinguishing the Belief in a Just World for Self Versus for Others." *Personality and Social Psychology Bulletin* 22:666.

London, T. 1997. "The Case Against Self-Esteem: Alternate Philosophies Toward Self That Would Raise the Probability of Pleasurable and Productive Living." *Journal of Rational-Emotive and Cognitive Behavior Therapy* 15:19.

Lu, L. 1996. "Coping Consistency and Emotional Outcome." *Personality and Individual Differences* 21:583.

Lu, L., and J. Shih. 1997. "Sources of Happiness: A Qualitative Approach." *Journal of Social Psychology* 137:181.

Lu, L., J. Shih, Y. Lin, and L. Ju. 1997. "Personal and Environmental Correlates of Happiness." *Personality and Individual Differences* 23:453.

Lundqvist, L., and U. Dimberg. 1995. "Facial Expressions Are Contagious." *Journal of Psychophysiology* 9:203.

Lykken, D., and A. Tellegen. 1996. "Happiness Is a Stochastic Phenomenon." *Psychological Science* 7:186.

Lyubomirsky, S. 1994. "The Hedonistic Consequences of Social Comparison: Implications for Enduring Happiness and Transient Mood." Ph.D. dissertation, Stanford University, Palo Alto, California.

Lyubomirsky, S., and L. Ross. 1997. "Hedonistic Consequences of Social Comparison." *Journal of Personality and Social Psychology* 73:1141.

Maddux, J. 1997. "Habit, Health, and Happiness." *Journal of Sport and Exercise Psychology* 19:331.

Madigan, M. J., D. Mise, and M. Maynard. 1996. "Life Satisfaction and Level of Activity." *Activities, Adaptation, and Aging* 21:21.

Magen, Z., M. Birenbaum, and D. Pery. 1996. "Experiencing Joy and Sorrow." *International Forum for Logotherapy* 19:45.

Mano, H. 1997. "Affect and Persuasion." *Psychology and Marketing* 14:315.

Marshall, G., M. Burnam, P. Koegel, and G. Sullivan. 1996. "Objective Life Circumstances and Life Satisfaction." *Journal of Health and Social Behavior* 37:44.

McGregor, I., and B. Little. 1998. "Personal Projects, Happiness, and Meaning: On Doing Well and Being Yourself." *Journal of Personality and Social Psychology* 74:494.

McIntosh, W., T. Harlow, and L. Martin. 1995. "Linkers and Nonlinkers: Goal Beliefs as a Moderator of the Effects of Everyday Hassles on Rumination, Depression, and Physical Complaints." *Journal of Applied Social Psychology* 25:1231.

Minetti, M. 1997. "Women's Educational Pursuits: Effects on Marital and Relationship Happiness." Master's thesis, University of Nevada, Las Vegas.

Monteiro, I. 1991. "Enrichment, Nurture, and Resource." Ph.D. dissertation, Catholic University of America, Washington, DC.

Mookherjee, H. 1997. "Perception of Well-Being Among Older Persons in Nonmetropolitan America." *Perceptual and Motor Skills* 85:943.

Murray, C., and M. J. Peacock. 1996. "A Model-Free Approach to the Study of Subjective Well-Being." In *Mental Health in Black America.* Thousand Oaks, CA: Sage.

177

Myers, D., and E. Diener. 1995. "Who Is Happy?" *Psychological Science* 6:10.

Neto, F. 1995. "Predictors of Satisfaction with Life." *Social Indicators Research* 35:93.

Ng, Y. 1996. "Happiness Surveys." *Social Indicators Research* 38:1.

Niedenthal, P., and J. Halberstadt. 1997. "Being Happy and Seeing Happy." *Cognition and Emotion* 11:403.

Noor, N. 1996. "Some Demographic, Personality, and Role Variables as Correlates of Women's Well-Being." *Sex Roles* 34:603.

Notarius, C. 1996. "Marriage: Will I Be Happy or Will I Be Sad?" In *A Lifetime of Relationships.* Pacific Grove, CA: Brooks/Cole.

Oates, W. 1997. "Reconciling with Unfulfilled Dreams at the End of Life." In *The Aging Family.* New York: Brunner/Mazel.

O'Connor, B. 1995. "Family and Friend Relationships Among Older and Younger Adults." *International Journal of Aging and Human Development* 40:9.

Oropesa, R. 1995. "Consumer Possessions, Consumer Passions, and Subjective Well-Being." *Sociological Forum* 10:215.

Otta, E., and F. Abrosio. 1996. "Reading a Smiling Face." *Perceptual and Motor Skills* 82:1111.

Panos, K. 1997. "Linking: An Exploration of Related Constructs and Effects on Happiness." Master's thesis, American University, Washington, DC.

Parducci, A. 1995. *Happiness, Pleasure, and Judgment: The Contextual Theory and Its Applications.* Mahwah, NJ: Erlbaum.

Parker, D. 1996. "The Relationship Between Time Spent by Older Adults in Leisure Activities and Life Satisfaction." *Physical and Occupational Therapy in Geriatrics* 14:61.

Parr, V. 1997. "How to Feel Good Without Feeling Good About Yourself." *Journal of Rational-Emotive and Cognitive Behavior Therapy* 15:5.

Pavot, W., F. Fujita, and E. Diener. 1997. "The Relation Between Self-Aspect Congruence, Personality, and Subjective Well-Being." *Personality and Individual Differences* 22:183.

Pegalis, L. 1994. "Frequency and Duration of Positive Affect: The Dispositionality of Happiness." Ph.D. dissertation, University of Georgia, Athens.

Pettijohn, T. 1996. "Perceived Happiness of College Students Measured by Maslow's Hierarchy of Needs." *Psychological Reports* 79:759.

Pilcher, J. 1998. "Affective and Daily Event Predictors of Life Satisfaction in College Students." *Social Indicators Research* 43:291.

Pilcher, J., and E. Ott. 1998. "The Relationship Between Sleep and Measures of Health and Well-Being in College Students: A Repeated Measures Approach." *Behavioral Medicine* 23:170.

Rahman, T., and A. Khaleque. 1996. "The Purpose in Life and Academic Behavior Problem Students." *Social Indicators Research* 39:59.

Ramanaiah, N., and F. Detwiler. 1997. "Life Satisfaction and the Five-Factor Model of Personality." *Psychological Reports* 80:1208.

Ramanaiah, N., F. Detwiler, and A. Byravan. 1995. "Sex-Role Orientation and Satisfaction with Life." *Psychological Reports* 71:1260.

Rogers, S. 1996. "Mothers' Work Hours and Marital Quality." *Journal of Marriage and the Family* 58:606.

Ruch, W., G. Koehler, and C. Van Thriel. 1997. "To Be in Good or Bad Humor." *Personality and Individual Differences* 22:477.

Scherpenzeel, A., and W. Saris. 1996. "Causal Direction in a Model of Life Satisfaction." *Social Indicators Research* 38:161.

Schyns, P. 1998. "Crossnational Differences in Happiness." *Social Indicators Research* 43:3.

Scope, E. 1999. "A Meta-Analysis of Research on Creativity." Ph.D. dissertation, Fordham University, New York, NY.

Scott, V. B., and W. D. McIntosh. 1999. "The Development of a Trait Measure of Ruminative Thought." *Personality & Individual Differences* 26:1045.

Seybolt, D., and M. Wagner. 1997. "Self-Reinforcement, Gender-Role, and Sex of Participant in Prediction of Life Satisfaction." *Psychological Reports* 81:519.

Shank, M., and F. Beasley. 1998. "Fan or Fanatic: Refining a Measure of Sports Involvement." *Journal of Sport Behavior* 21:435.

Sheehan, E. 1995. "Affective Responses to Employee Turnover." *Journal of Social Psychology* 135:63.

Sherer, M. 1996. "The Impact of Using Personal Computers on the Lives of Nursing Home Residents." *Physical and Occupational Therapy in Geriatrics* 14:13.

Simpson, R. 1990. "Conflict Styles and Social Network Relations as Predictors of Marital Happiness." Ph.D. dissertation, University of Michigan, Ann Arbor.

Sirgy, M. J., D. Cole, R. Kosenko, and H. L. Meadow. 1995. "A Life Satisfaction Measure." *Social Indicators Research* 34:237.

Smail, D. 1995. "Power and the Origins of Unhappiness." *Journal of Community and Applied Social Psychology* 5:347.

Smith, R. 1997. "Experiencing Negative Affect." Master's thesis, American University, Washington, DC.

Solomon, J. 1996. "Humor and Aging Well." *American Behavior Scientist* 39:249.

Staats, S., M. Armstrong-Stassen, and C. Partillo. 1995. "Student Well-Being: Are They Better Off Now?" *Social Indicators Research* 34:93.

Sugarman, S. 1997. "Happiness and Population Density." Master's thesis, California State University, Long Beach.

Suh, E., E. Diener, and F. Fujita. 1996. "Events and Subjective Well-Being: Only Recent Events Matter." *Journal of Personality and Social Psychology* 70:1091.

Takahashi, K., J. Tamura, and M. Tokoro. 1997. "Patterns of Social Relationships and Psychological Well-Being Among the Elderly." *International Journal of Behavioral Development* 21:417.

Taylor, C. 1988. "Assessment of Happiness Among Young Adults." Ph.D. dissertation, Iowa State University, Ames.

Tepperman, L., and J. Curtis. 1995. "A Life Satisfaction Scale for Use with National Adult Samples from the USA, Canada, and Mexico." *Social Indicators Research* 35:255.

Thakar, G., and G. Misra. 1995. "Correlates of Daily Hassles Among Dual Career Women." *Journal of the Academy of Applied Psychology* 21:93.

Thurman, C. 1981. "Personality Correlates of the Type A Behavior Pattern." Ph.D. dissertation, University of Georgia, Athens.

Tom, G., T. Schmidt, and M. Deuber. 1995. "The Materialistic Orientation of Business Students." *College Student Journal* 29:106.

Turner, C. 1994. "Follow Through in Conflict Resolution as a Factor in Marital Satisfaction and Personal Happiness." Master's thesis, University of Nevada, Las Vegas.

Van Dijk, W., and J. Van Der Pligt. 1997. "The Impact of Probability and Magnitude of Outcome on Disappointment and Elation." *Organizational Behavior and Human Decision Processes* 69:277.

Van Overwalle, F., I. Mervielde, and J. De Schuyter. 1995. "Structural Modeling of the Relationships Between Attributional Dimensions, Emotions, and Performance of College Freshmen." *Cognition and Emotion* 9:59.

Veenhoven, R. 1996. "Developments in Satisfaction Research." *Social Indicators Research* 37:1.

Voydanoff, P., and B. Donnelly. 1998. "Parents' Risk and Protective Factors as Prediction of Parental Well-Being and Behavior." *Journal of Marriage and the Family* 60:344.

Warburton, D. 1995. "Effects of Caffeine on Cognition and Mood Without Caffeine Abstinence." *Psychopharmacology* 119:66.

West, C., D. Reed, and G. Gildengorin. 1998. "Can Money Buy Happiness?" *Journal of the American Geriatrics Society* 46:49.

Williams, A., D. Haber, G. Weaver, and J. Freeman. 1998. "Altruistic Activity." *Activities, Adaptation, and Aging* 22:31.

Wilson, S., C. Henry, and G. Peterson. 1997. "Life Satisfaction Among Low-Income Rural Youth in Appalachia." *Journal of Adolescence* 20:443.

Wrzesniewski, A., C. McCauley, P. Rozin, and B. Schwartz. 1997. "Jobs, Careers, and Callings: People's Relations to Their Work." *Journal of Research in Personality* 31:21.

Wu, P. 1998. "Goal Structures of Materialists vs. Non-Materialists." Ph.D. dissertation, University of Michigan, Ann Arbor.

Acknowledgments

I am grateful for the fine work of Gideon Weil and the staff at Harper San Francisco who have helped to make this book a better tool for its readers.

I also thank my agents, Maureen Lasher and Eric Lasher, whose interest and faith in this project were invaluable.

THE
SIMPLE SCIENCE OF A GREAT LIFE

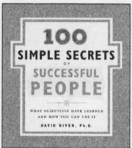

This bestselling series of scientifically based advice offers practical guidance on the most important aspects of our lives—happiness, success, relationships, and health. With close to a million copies sold, the Simple Secrets series takes the most valuable scientific research and delivers it in fun, easily digestible findings complete with real-world examples that people can use in their daily lives.

**100 SIMPLE SECRETS
OF GREAT RELATIONSHIPS**
ISBN 0-06-115790-2

**100 SIMPLE SECRETS
OF SUCCESSFUL PEOPLE**
ISBN 0-06-115793-7

**SIMPLE SECRETS FOR BECOMING
HEALTHY, WEALTHY, AND WISE**
ISBN 0-06-085881-8

Now available in your bookstore.

HarperSanFrancisco
A Division of HarperCollinsPublishers